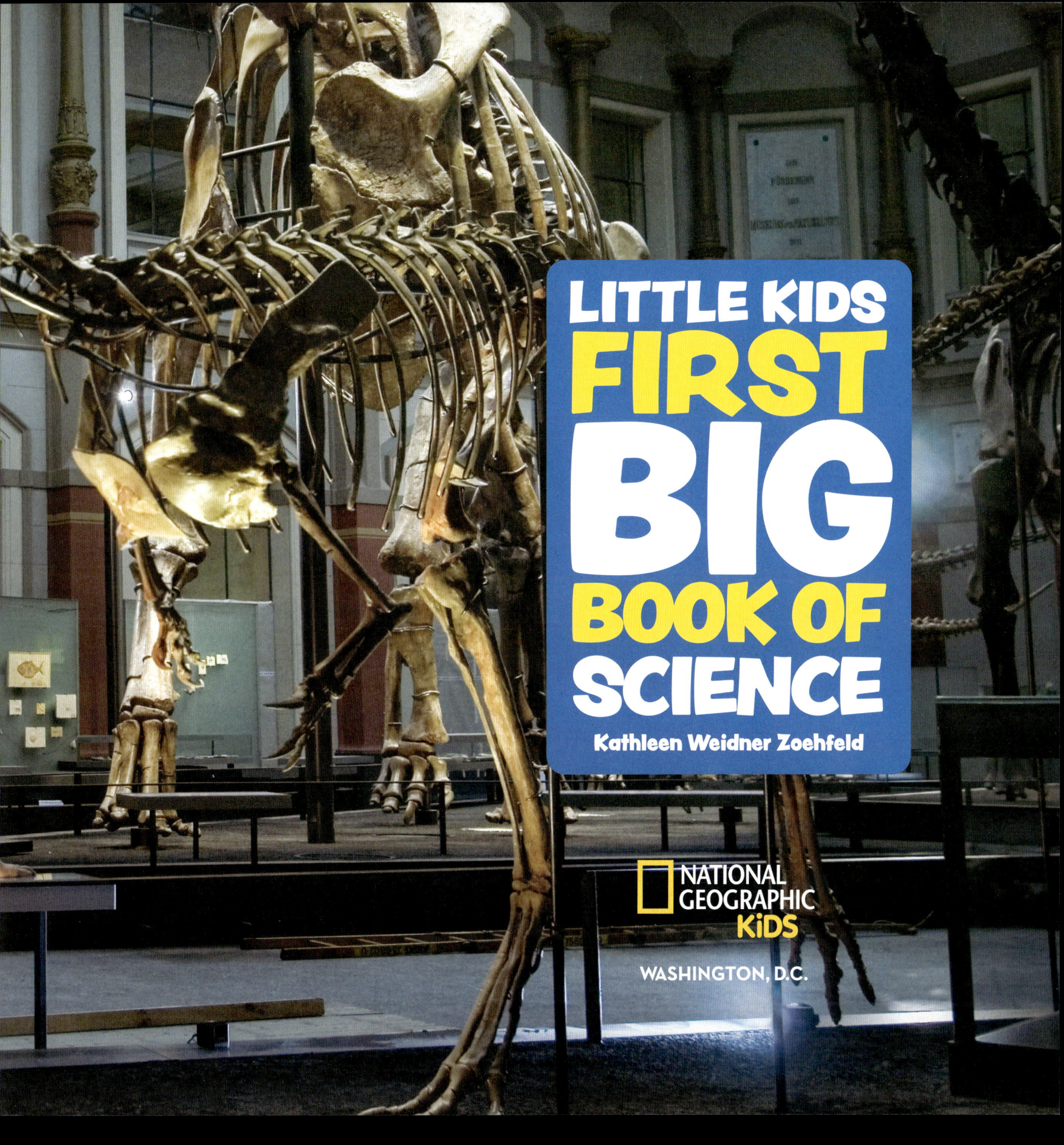

CONTENTS

INTRODUCTION 6
HOW TO USE THIS BOOK 7

CHAPTER ONE
WHAT IS SCIENCE? 8
  ASKING QUESTIONS 10
  YOUR SENSES 12
  FINDING ANSWERS 14
  KEEPING A JOURNAL 16
  SHARING WHAT YOU LEARN ... 18
  KINDS OF SCIENTISTS 20
  BRANCHES OF SCIENCE 22
  WORLD OF KNOWLEDGE 24

CHAPTER TWO
LIFE SCIENCE 26
  ALL LIVING THINGS 28
  THE HUMAN BODY 30
  ALL ABOUT ANIMALS 34
  THE INSECT WORLD 36
  TRY THIS! 39
  CRITTERS WITH SHELLS 40
  SWIMMING WITH FISH 42
  AMPHIBIANS AND REPTILES .. 44
  FEATHERS AND WINGS 48
  TRY THIS! 51
  FURRY ANIMALS 52
  TRY THIS! 55
  PLANTING SEEDS 56
  TRY THIS! 57
  GROWING FOOD 58
  NATURE'S NEIGHBORHOODS . 60
  EXPLORING YOUR
    NEIGHBORHOOD 64

CHAPTER THREE

EARTH AND SPACE   66
- PLANET EARTH   68
- ROCKY WORLD   70
- TRY THIS!   72
- DIGGING UP THE PAST   74
- VOLCANOES   78
- EARTHQUAKE POWER   80
- DEEP BLUE OCEAN   82
- WATCHING THE WEATHER   86
- TRY THIS!   89
- RISING TEMPERATURES   90
- OUTER SPACE   92

CHAPTER FOUR

PHYSICAL SCIENCE   96
- EVERYTHING IS MATTER   98
- MIX AND STIR   100
- MOVING FORCES   104
- WAVES OF SOUND   106
- TRY THIS!   107
- WAVES OF LIGHT   108
- IT'S SHOCKING!   110
- TRY THIS!   112

CHAPTER FIVE

GREAT INVENTIONS   114
- TRY, TRY AGAIN   116
- TYPES OF ENGINEERS   118
- PROBLEM-SOLVING   120

PARENT TIPS   122
GLOSSARY   124
ADDITIONAL RESOURCES   126
INDEX   126
CREDITS   128

INTRODUCTION

In these pages, young readers get an exciting tour of the main branches of science. The questions scientists ask are much like the questions children ask every day. This book shows kids how scientists go about finding answers. Activities sprinkled throughout encourage readers to keep a science journal and begin some science experiments of their own.

CHAPTER ONE provides an introduction to science and the scientific process. A simple example shows kids that they already think like scientists as they observe their world, ask questions, come up with hypotheses, and look for answers.

CHAPTER TWO focuses on the life sciences. Readers see biologists, botanists, and zoologists at work, observing Earth's amazing variety of animals and plants.

CHAPTER THREE explores all aspects of planet Earth—from the rocks beneath our feet to the clouds in the sky above. It shows astronomers learning about other planets, oceanographers diving into the sea, and geologists delving into mysteries deep inside the Earth.

CHAPTER FOUR is about the material world that kids experience all around them. Here they learn how chemists mix substances to make new substances and how physicists observe the way things move.

CHAPTER FIVE takes a look at how engineers use knowledge from all branches of science to solve problems and create useful inventions.

HOW TO USE THIS BOOK

Colorful **PHOTOGRAPHS** illustrate science and scientists in action on each spread.

POP-UP FACTS sprinkled throughout provide additional information about the main text.

FACT BOXES help young readers learn the names of the main branches of science, the types of scientists who work in those fields, and what aspects of the world they study.

Interactive **QUESTIONS** in each chapter encourage conversation related to the main topics.

MORE FOR PARENTS in the back of the book offers parent tips that include fun activities that encourage kids to think like scientists. There's also a helpful glossary.

CHAPTER 1
WHAT IS SCIENCE?

This chapter introduces you to the way scientists observe and think about the world and how they go about finding answers. Read on to find out how you can be a scientist, too.

ASKING QUESTIONS

Science is a special way of learning about the world. If you wonder about the world and ask a lot of questions, you are already thinking like a scientist! Some questions are easy to answer. Others are hard. But science can help answer almost any question you ask.

WHAT does my **KITTEN** need to **HELP HIM GROW?**

HOW FAR AWAY is the **MOON?**

WHAT IS SCIENCE?

WILL it RAIN TODAY?

HOW can I make my CAR GO FASTER?

HOW can this LITTLE SEED GROW into a great BIG TREE?

YOUR SENSES

You begin learning when you use your senses. You use these senses every day. Scientists call this kind of learning "observation."

When you observe the world around you, you discover new things. Those new things can lead to a lot of interesting questions.

You use your **EYES** to **SEE.**

You use your **EARS** to **HEAR.**

WHAT IS SCIENCE?

You use your **HANDS** to **TOUCH**.

You use your **TONGUE** to **TASTE**.

You use your **NOSE** to **SMELL**.

FINDING ANSWERS

To find answers to questions, scientists follow a few important steps. You can look for answers the same way a scientist does.

Once you have a question, the next step is to think about what the answer might be. You use information and knowledge you already have. You might come up with two or three possible answers—or even more. The answer you think is best is your hypothesis.

However, just thinking an answer is right doesn't mean for sure that it is right. A scientist takes another step. She must *prove* that her answer is right. To do that, she sets up an experiment.

RULER

An **EXPERIMENT** is a kind of **TEST** that shows whether a **HYPOTHESIS** is correct.

WHAT IS SCIENCE?

SCALE

SCIENTISTS use tools such as **RULERS** and **SCALES** to find out exactly how **LONG** or how **HEAVY** something is.

GUINEA PIGS

As part of her experiment, a scientist may need to keep track of how much bigger one of her guinea pigs is than the other. She uses a scale to weigh them. She uses a ruler to measure them from snout to tail. When a scientist does an experiment, she keeps track of all her observations in her science journal.

KEEPING A JOURNAL

When you do your own experiments, you can write notes or draw pictures in a science journal, too. That way you can show others what you did and what you learned.

Something that **CAN BE CHANGED** in an experiment (such as how much sugar you use) is called a **VARIABLE.**

Science Journal

What I Observed: I mixed lemon juice with water to make lemonade. It is very sour. Yuck!

My Big Question: How can I make my lemonade sweeter?

My Hypothesis: Sugar is sweet. If I add sugar, I think the lemonade will taste sweeter.

My Experiment:

1. I poured one cup of lemonade into a glass and the exact same amount into another glass.

2. I stirred one teaspoon of sugar into one glass of lemonade.

MEASURING SPOONS

WHAT IS SCIENCE?

3. I tasted the lemonade in each glass to compare the lemonade without sugar to the one with sugar.

What Happened: The lemonade with sugar was sweeter than the lemonade without sugar.

What I Learned: Sugar makes lemonade sweet.

My Next Question Is: What would happen if I added two teaspoons of sugar to the lemonade?

The glass of lemonade with **NO ADDED** sugar is called a **CONTROL**. A control is the part of an experiment that stays **UNCHANGED.**

MEASURING CUPS

SHARING WHAT YOU LEARN

When your experiment is done, it's fun to share your new knowledge. If one of your friends doesn't believe that adding sugar made the lemonade taste so delicious, you can show her your experiment. She can also do the experiment herself. If she gets the same result, it means your hypothesis is probably right.

Other friends can try the experiment, too. The more people who try your experiment and tell you that the sugar made the lemonade sweeter, the more certain you can be about your hypothesis.

In **SCIENCE**, a **HYPOTHESIS** that has been tested and accepted is called a **THEORY**.

WHAT IS SCIENCE?

SALT

Other scientists may come up with different hypotheses. One person might think salt will make lemonade sweeter. Another may want to try honey. If you do an experiment and your hypothesis turns out to be wrong, don't worry! That just means you've learned something important: You've discovered one thing that doesn't work.

HONEY

All the weights and other **MEASUREMENTS** a scientist **WRITES DOWN** while doing an experiment are called **DATA**.

KINDS OF SCIENTISTS

The world is a very big place, filled with many interesting things to do and amazing places to explore. It takes a lot of different kinds of scientists to study all the different parts of the natural world. Here are just a few.

CHEMIST

VOLCANOLOGIST

If you could spend a day with one of these scientists, who would you choose?

WHAT IS SCIENCE?

ZOOLOGIST

ASTRONOMER

METEOROLOGIST

Some **SCIENTISTS** work in **LABS,** and some **EXPLORE** dangerous places. Others learn about **ANIMALS** or **PLANTS,** or study Earth's **AIR, WATER,** or **ROCKS.** Some look into **SPACE** to make new discoveries.

BRANCHES OF SCIENCE

Think of science as a tree. Imagine that science is the trunk of the tree. The tree's branches represent the many kinds of science that exist.

One of the main branches of the tree is for all living things: BIOLOGY. Coming from that is a branch that deals with animals: ZOOLOGY. Off of that branch are smaller branches that represent the different animal sciences.

For example, there is a branch for insects, and another for birds. Each of these branches of science has a name, such as entomology for insects and ornithology for birds. You'll discover what the other names mean as you read this book.

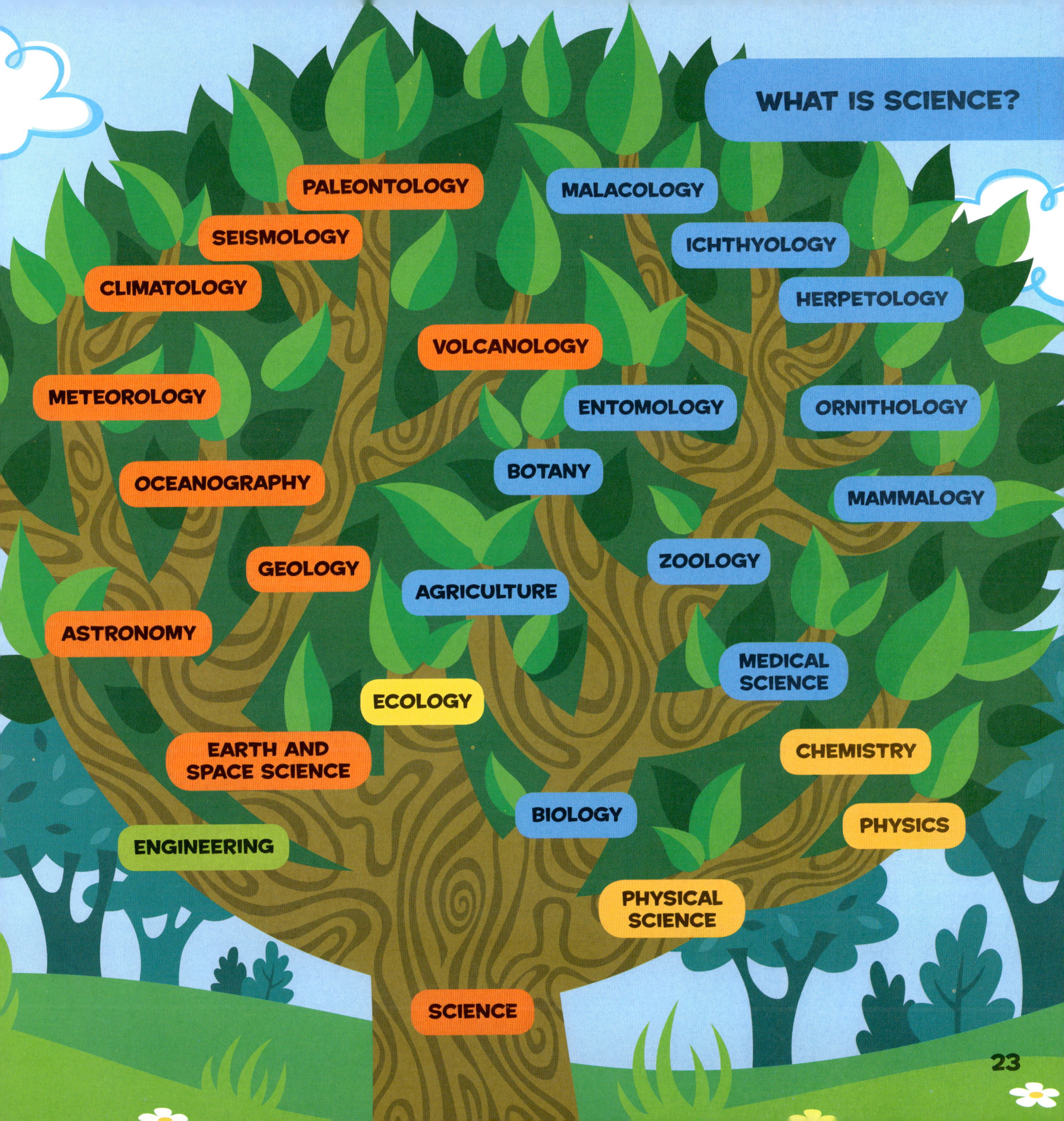

WORLD OF KNOWLEDGE

The space shuttle *DISCOVERY* blasted off into space using **ROCKET POWER.**

By asking questions and then using scientific observation and experimentation, scientists have made a lot of great discoveries. When scientists find answers to big questions, the answers become part of our knowledge.

WHAT IS SCIENCE?

VETERINARIAN

Veterinarians **TAKE CARE** of all kinds of animals, from **DOGS** and **CATS** to **BIRDS** and **HORSES**.

Scientific knowledge makes it possible to fly in spaceships, drive cars, talk on the phone, play video games, use a computer, keep animals and people safe and healthy, grow good food, and much more.

Anyone can be a scientist and discover new things. Let's find out more about the different kinds of science, what scientists do, and all the amazing things they wonder about and learn.

CHAPTER 2
LIFE SCIENCE

Plants, animals, and people—Earth is filled with an amazing variety of living things. In this chapter, you will learn about the many different kinds of life scientists.

ALL LIVING THINGS

From tiny bugs to giant whales, millions of different kinds of creatures live on Earth. All of them are the same in a few important ways. All living things, including plants, grow and move. They need food for energy. They need water. Most need oxygen to breathe.

MONARCH BUTTERFLY CATERPILLAR

FACTS

BIOLOGY
(by-AH-luh-jee) the science of all living things

BIOLOGIST
a scientist who studies living things

LIVING THINGS
includes plants and animals

OXYGEN is a gas in the air we **BREATHE.** Oxygen is also in **WATER.**

LIFE SCIENCE

Living things are different from each other in many ways, too. Because there are so many kinds of living things, a biologist usually chooses one kind to learn the most about.

HUMPBACK WHALE

BEETLE

A **HAND LENS** makes **SMALL** things look **BIGGER.**

MOUSE

THE HUMAN BODY

Sometimes the doctor may give you a **SHOT**, or **VACCINATION**. Shots help your body fight off many types of **GERMS** that could make you sick.

Achoo! You sneeze and sniffle and cough. You feel achy and shivery. Time to visit the doctor!

She tells you to open your mouth and say *ahhh*. She holds down your tongue with a tongue depressor and looks at your throat. She takes your temperature with a thermometer and listens to your heart and lungs using a stethoscope.

STETHOSCOPE

FACTS

MEDICAL SCIENCE
the science of the human body—a branch of biology

DOCTOR
a medical scientist who helps people stay healthy and helps heal them when they are hurt or sick

LIFE SCIENCE

You get **WEIGHED** and **MEASURED** at the doctor's office to make sure you are **GROWING WELL.**

TONGUE DEPRESSORS

THERMOMETER

Using medical science, your doctor figures out what has made you sick. She says you have a virus. The virus is a type of germ that caused you to feel sick. The doctor may give you some medicine that will help you feel better.

Doctors have to study all about the human body, from head to toe. They learn about the outside of the body—the skin. They also learn about the bones, muscles, and organs inside the body, like the heart and stomach.

There are more than **200 BONES** in the human body. The **BIGGEST** is the **THIGHBONE**, in your upper leg. The **SMALLEST** is a tiny bone inside your ear.

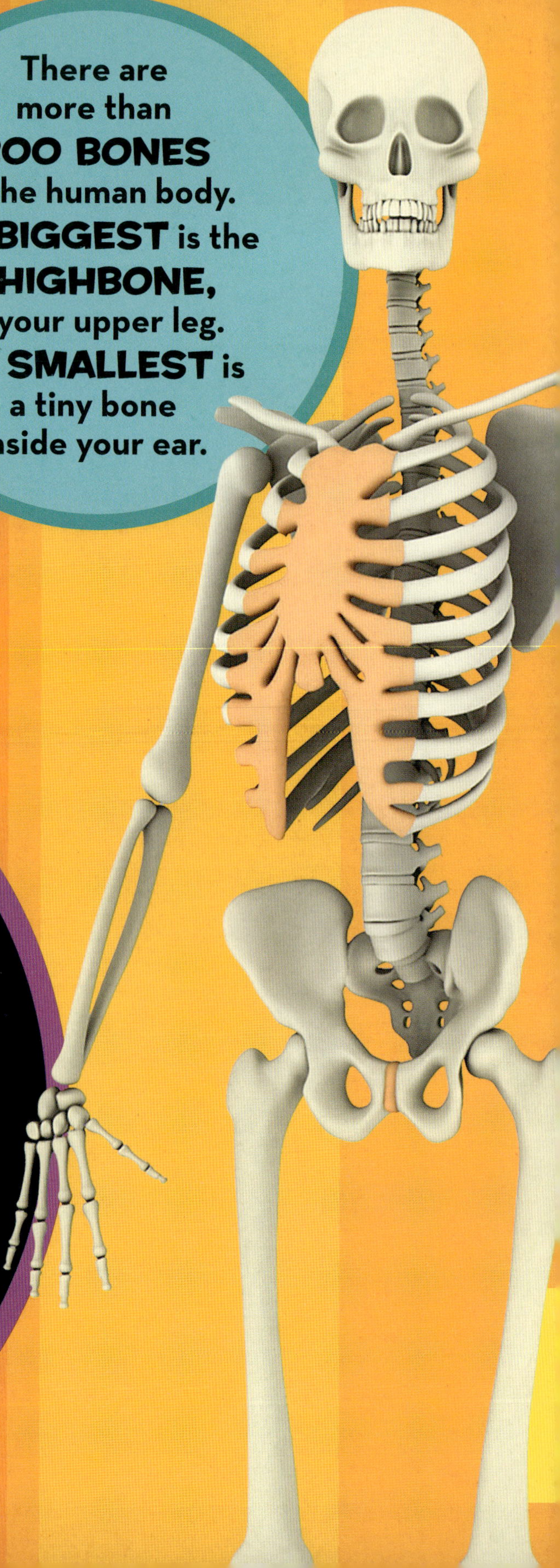

A doctor uses an **X-RAY MACHINE** to see your **BONES** if he thinks you may have a **BROKEN** one.

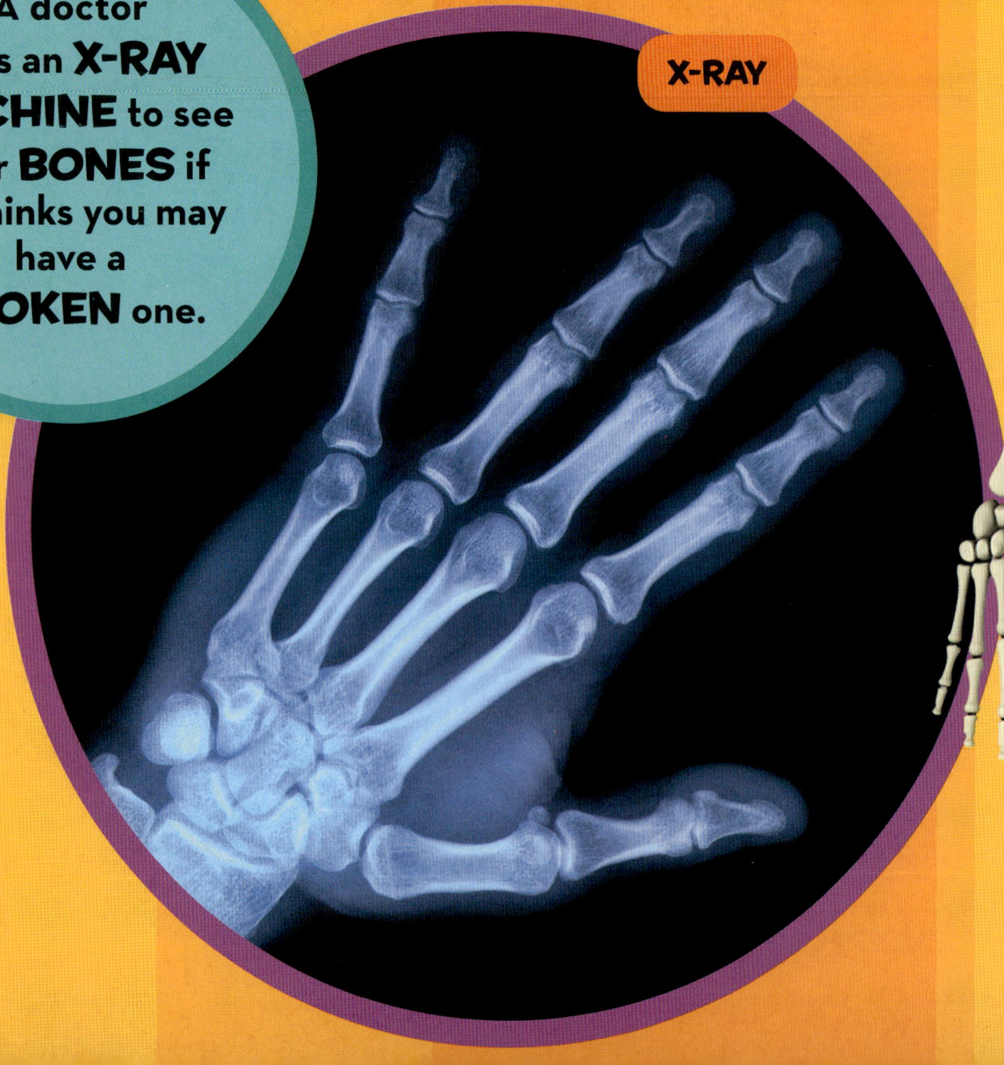

X-RAY

LIFE SCIENCE

If the x-ray shows you have a **BROKEN BONE**, the doctor may put a **CAST** on that body part to hold the bone in place while it **HEALS**.

CAST

Many doctors pick one part of the body to study in depth. Some doctors specialize in the human heart. Others focus on how people digest their food. One kind of doctor helps patients with ear, nose, and throat problems. There is a special kind of doctor for almost every part of a person's body.

X-RAY MACHINE

Which part of the body would you like to learn more about? Why?

ALL ABOUT ANIMALS

Doctors and veterinarians use observation skills to help keep their patients healthy. Zoologists learn about wild animals by observing them. When you take a walk in your neighborhood, hike in the woods, or visit a zoo, you can observe animals yourself. You can see them, hear them, and sometimes even smell them!

CHAMELEON

PANDA

FACTS

ZOOLOGY
(zo-AH-luh-jee) the science of animals—a branch of biology

ZOOLOGIST
a biologist who studies animals

LIFE SCIENCE

SCARLET MACAWS

Some animals fly in the air. Some swim in water. Some burrow in the ground or crawl up trees. There are many different kinds of animals, so zoologists sort them into groups. The groups are based on body types and on how the animals live and grow.

The word **"ZOO"** comes from the Greek word that means **"ANIMAL."**

RED-EYED TREE FROG

GIRAFFE

THE INSECT WORLD

CHRYSALIS

MONARCH BUTTERFLY

A small chrysalis hangs from a twig. You see the chrysalis wiggle and shake. Like a scientist, you wonder what is happening. So you keep watching. The chrysalis splits open and a butterfly begins to unfold its new wings. You have observed part of the life cycle of a butterfly.

If you draw the chrysalis and the butterfly in your science journal, you can share your new knowledge with your family and friends.

FACTS

ENTOMOLOGY
(en-tuh-MA-luh-jee)
the science of insects—
a branch of zoology

ENTOMOLOGIST
a zoologist who studies insects

INSECTS
have six legs; an exoskeleton—a hard shell-like covering on the outside of the body; three main body parts

LIFE SCIENCE

DRAGONFLY

HEAD
THORAX
ABDOMEN

Many kinds of **INSECTS** have **WINGS** for **FLYING.**

Like all insects, this **ANT** has **THREE** main body parts.

Animals with **SKELETONS** on the **INSIDE** of their bodies are called **VERTEBRATES.** Animals **WITHOUT SKELETONS** inside their bodies, such as insects, are called **INVERTEBRATES.**

CICADA

37

Spiders have exoskeletons, just like insects. But they are not insects. What's the difference?

Observe this spider closely. How many legs does it have? You've found the difference! All spiders have eight legs. All insects have six legs.

GOLDEN ORB WEAVER

TRY THIS!

Some insects live on grass, leaves, or branches. Others live on the ground or burrow under it. Many insects can fly. An entomologist looks for insects in all kinds of places. Can you find all the insects in this picture?

ANSWER: There are seven—field cricket, fiery searcher beetle, green darner dragonfly, stinkbug, silvery blue butterfly, Western blood-red lady beetle, Western tiger swallowtail butterfly

SEASHELLS come in many **SIZES, COLORS,** and **SHAPES.**

FACTS

MALACOLOGY (mah-lah-CAH-luh-jee) the science of mollusks, a group of animals that includes shelled animals such as clams and snails—a branch of zoology

MALACOLOGIST a zoologist who studies mollusks

CRITTERS WITH SHELLS

You walk barefoot in the sand at the beach. Ocean waves gently lap the shore. All of a sudden—*ouch!* You step on something hard and pointy. You pick it up with your hands and feel all its bumps and swirls. It's a seashell that has washed up onto the beach from the ocean.

LIFE SCIENCE

SCALLOP

CLAMS

CLAMS and **SCALLOPS** have two shells that are **HELD TOGETHER** by a **HINGE.**

A kind of soft-bodied animal called a mollusk once lived in the shell. A hard shell helps protect a soft animal from hungry predators.

Octopuses are a special kind of **MOLLUSK** without a hard outer shell. They are good at **HIDE-AND-SEEK.** An octopus can **CHANGE COLOR** to **BLEND** in with its surroundings.

OCTOPUS

41

SWIMMING WITH FISH

It's fun to watch fish swimming in a fishbowl. Ichthyologists enjoy watching fish, too. They keep fish in huge aquariums. They also study fish in streams, rivers, lakes, and oceans.

To find fish in the wild, ichthyologists swim underwater. Unlike fish, people can't breathe underwater. Ichthyologists wear diving gear with special air tanks for breathing.

An ichthyologist often picks one species of fish to watch over a long time. The scientist discovers how the fish find food, how far they swim, and where they hang out to feel safe. There are thousands of different species, or kinds, of fish. New species are discovered every year.

FACTS

ICHTHYOLOGY
(ick-thee-AH-luh-jee) the science of fish—a branch of zoology

ICHTHYOLOGIST
a zoologist who studies fish

FISH
are vertebrates; have gills for taking in oxygen underwater and fins for swimming

LIFE SCIENCE

AIR TANK

WET SUIT

The **WHALE SHARK** is not a whale. It is the **BIGGEST** kind of **FISH** in the world. It lives in the **OCEAN.**

RAYS are a kind of fish. They **FLAP THEIR FINS** or move their bodies up and down to **SWIM.**

Where are some places that you have seen fish?

AMPHIBIANS AND REPTILES

SALAMANDER

Do you ever wonder what kinds of animals live under rocks? If you peek underneath one, you might see insects and worms, and maybe even a salamander. Salamanders are amphibians. During the sunny part of the day, salamanders like to hide in dark, moist places.

FACTS

HERPETOLOGY
(herp-eh-TOL-uh-jee) the science of reptiles and amphibians—a branch of zoology

HERPETOLOGIST
a zoologist who studies reptiles and amphibians

REPTILES
are vertebrates; have dry, scaly skin; most lay eggs on land

AMPHIBIANS
are vertebrates; have smooth, moist (sometimes slimy) skin; most lay eggs in water

LIFE SCIENCE

TADPOLE

NET

A **TADPOLE** is a **BABY FROG.** As it becomes an adult frog, it **GROWS LEGS** for **HOPPING** on land.

Can you name three ways you look different from when you were a baby?

Herpetologists have discovered that many kinds of amphibians take in air through their skin. Amphibians need to keep their skin moist in order to breathe. That's one clue that will help you figure out the best places to look for salamanders and other amphibians.

TREE FROG

FROGS and **TOADS** are **AMPHIBIANS.**

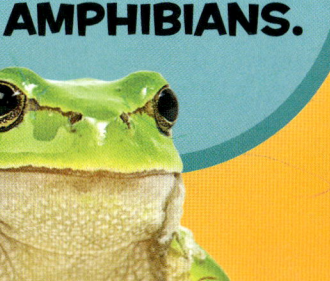

45

Snakes, lizards, turtles, and crocodiles are reptiles. Reptiles breathe air using their lungs. Amphibians have jellylike eggs that must stay wet. Reptile eggs have tough, leathery shells and do not need to be wet.

Reptiles don't need to stay close to water. They live on dry land most of their lives. Herpetologists find reptiles in all kinds of places—in trees, in burrows, near swamps and rivers, and even gliding through the air!

NILE CROCODILE

The **NILE CROCODILE** can **WEIGH** as much as a **PIANO**.

LIFE SCIENCE

The **EMERALD TREE BOA** lives in treetops in South American rain forests. Adults are **EMERALD GREEN**, while the babies, like this one, are **ORANGE** or **BRICK RED** in color.

TURTLES have skeletons inside their bodies. They also have **SHELLS** on the outside to help **PROTECT** them.

A **FLYING LIZARD** doesn't fly like a bird. Instead, it fans out two folded flaps of skin, which are supported by its ribs. It uses these skin flaps like **WINGS** to **GLIDE** from tree to tree.

PAINTED TURTLE

FEATHERS AND WINGS

Early in the morning, you hear a bird singing outside. *Cheer-up, cheerily, cheer-up*. What kind is it? You grab a pair of binoculars. Following the sound, you spot the bird in a tree. It's a robin. The next time you hear that song, you'll know what kind of bird is nearby.

ROBIN

FACTS

ORNITHOLOGY
(or-nih-THAH-luh-jee) the science of birds—a branch of zoology

ORNITHOLOGIST
a zoologist who studies birds

BIRDS
are vertebrates; have feathers, a beak, two legs, and two wings

LIFE SCIENCE

KING BIRD OF PARADISE

GENTOO PENGUIN

There are **39 different SPECIES** of **BIRDS OF PARADISE.**

Ornithologists observe birds the same way, using binoculars and spotting scopes—and their ears! Around the world, ornithologists have identified more than 10,000 species of birds—from penguins in Antarctica to birds of paradise in the Indonesian rain forest.

BINOCULARS make faraway things look **CLOSER.** They help you **OBSERVE** animals **AT A DISTANCE** without disturbing them.

Ornithologists do more than identify species and study birds' songs and calls. They study what birds eat and how they raise their young. From season to season, these scientists keep track of when and where birds migrate. And they give the best advice about what kind of food to use in your bird feeders!

Most birds **BUILD NESTS** for their **EGGS** and **RAISE THEIR CHICKS** there.

BLACK-NAPED BLUE FLYCATCHER

Some **BIRD SPECIES** live in one place all year. Others, like these **SNOW GEESE, MIGRATE.** They move to warmer places during the **WINTER MONTHS.**

If you could be a bird, what colors would you like your feathers to be?

TRY THIS!

Can you point out these bird body parts?

- FEATHERS
- BEAK
- LEGS
- WINGS
- HEAD
- TAIL

GREEN VIOLET-EAR HUMMINGBIRD

FURRY ANIMALS

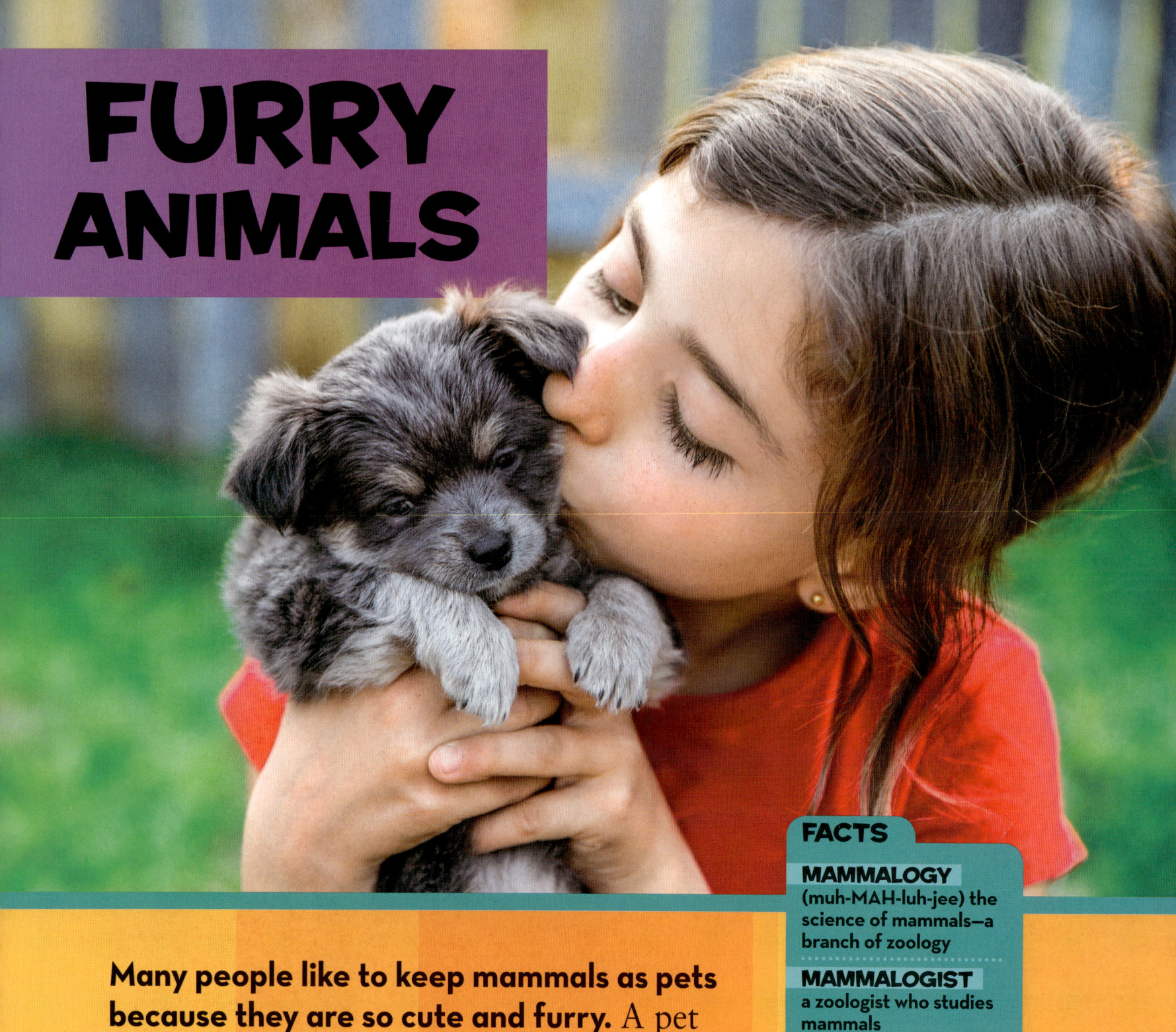

Many people like to keep mammals as pets because they are so cute and furry. A pet dog is a mammal. So is a cat or a hamster. And so are you!

FACTS

MAMMALOGY (muh-MAH-luh-jee) the science of mammals—a branch of zoology

MAMMALOGIST a zoologist who studies mammals

MAMMALS are vertebrates; feed their babies milk from their own bodies; have hair or fur

LIFE SCIENCE

ECHIDNA

PLATYPUS

Most **MAMMALS GIVE BIRTH** to live young. But two kinds of mammals **LAY EGGS**: the **ECHIDNA** and the **PLATYPUS**. They live in the wild in Australia.

You can observe your pet, just like a mammalogist would observe a mammal in the wild. You can use a camera to get photos of your pet. Photos can help you record changes from one day to the next.

This big male **MOUNTAIN GORILLA** lives in a national park in **RWANDA**. There are only a few hundred of these animals left in the world. **MAMMALOGISTS** are looking for ways to protect them.

ELEPHANT

Mammalogists have many questions about mammals in the wild. Where do they prefer to live? How do they grow? How do they find their food?

Like other zoologists, mammalogists often choose one kind of mammal to study over a long period of time. Sometimes they even live in the wild to observe animals such as gorillas, elephants, wolves, or leopards up close.

What wild animal would you most like to study? Why?

TRY THIS!

Mammals come in many shapes and sizes. Use the clues to name the different mammals.

Sharp claws and teeth help this mammal hunt. A male has a mane of fur around its face.

With its long neck, this mammal can reach yummy leaves, even on the highest branches.

Strong, chisel-like teeth help this mammal gnaw down trees to build dams.

This mammal has some bristly hairs on its body. It also has the longest nose of any animal.

This mammal lives and hunts in a group called a pack.

This mammal is very small. It may like to hide in your house.

ANSWERS: 1. lion, 2. giraffe, 3. beaver, 4. elephant, 5. wolf, 6. mouse

PLANTING SEEDS

Plants don't run and jump and play like animals do. But plants are living things, too. Like all living things, they grow, and they need water and oxygen. Green plants don't have to eat the way we do, though. They make their own food, using energy from the sun. Most plants slowly bend or move a little bit, to keep their leaves in the sun.

FACTS

BOTANY (BAH-tuh-nee) the science of plants—a branch of biology

BOTANIST a biologist who studies plants

MOST PLANTS have roots, stems, and leaves

SEEDS are usually formed **INSIDE** a plant's **FLOWERS.**

FLOWER

LEAF

STEM

ROOTS

TRY THIS!

Grow a Plant From a Seed

YOU'LL NEED
- a seed
- a flowerpot or cup with a small hole in the bottom (to let extra water drain out)
- soil
- water
- a sunny window

Fill your pot with soil.

Push the seed into the soil, about 1/2 inch deep.

Cover the seed with soil.

Moisten the soil with water.

Place your pot on a sunny windowsill. Then, watch and wait! It will take a few days for your seed to sprout. Check your flowerpot each day and make sure the soil is moist.

Once your plant sprouts, you can use a ruler to measure how much it grows each day. Be sure to mark down your observations in your science journal.

GROWING FOOD

All living things need food, and all our food comes from other living things. In the wild, animals search for plants to eat or they hunt for other animals to eat.

Most food for people is grown or raised on farms. Agricultural scientists try to figure out better ways of raising our food.

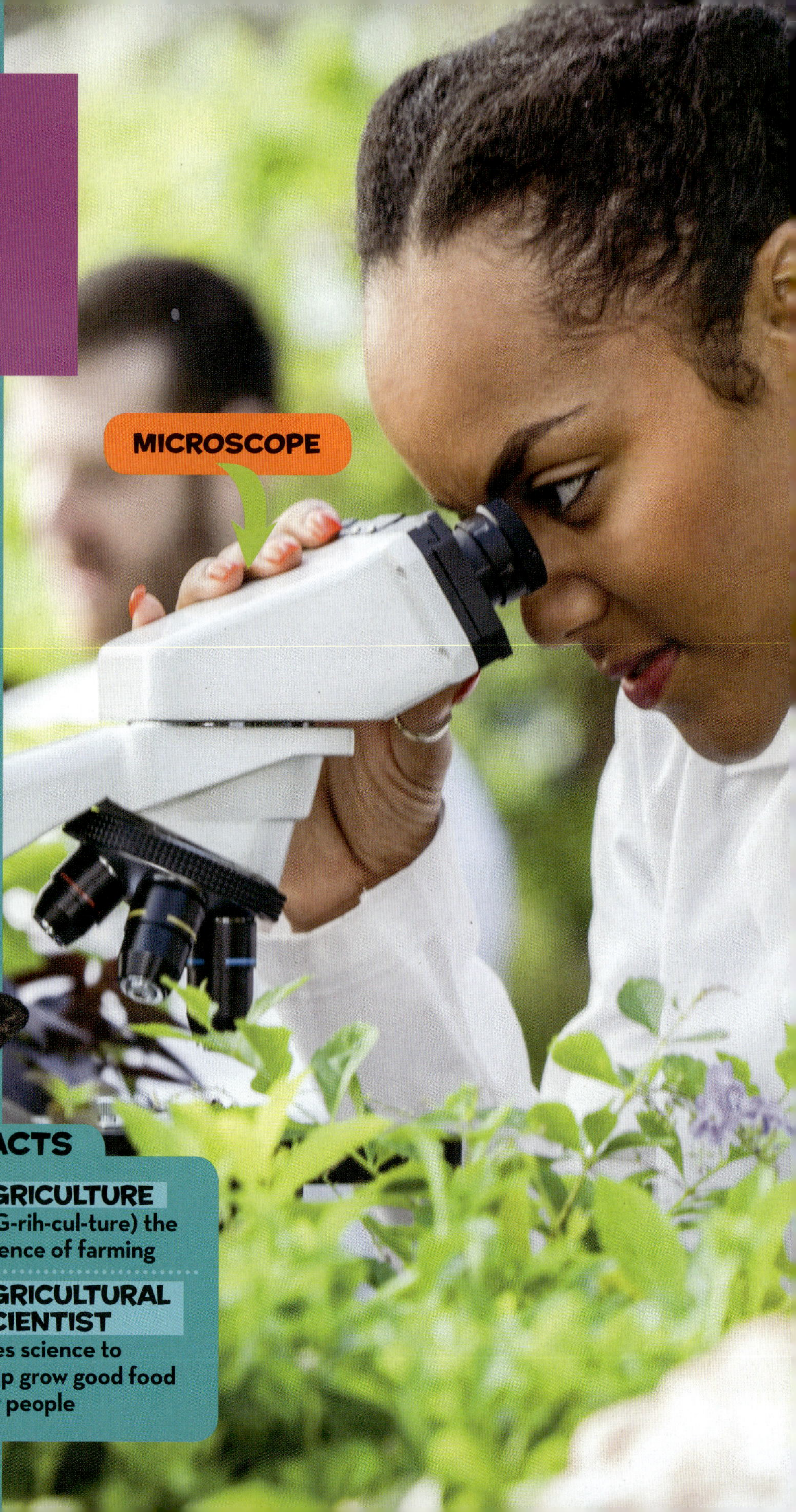

MICROSCOPE

DAIRY COW

FACTS

AGRICULTURE (AG-rih-cul-ture) the science of farming

AGRICULTURAL SCIENTIST uses science to help grow good food for people

LIFE SCIENCE

WORMS live in **SOIL.** They help keep soil **HEALTHY** and good for growing **PLANTS.**

STRAWBERRIES

Some of our food comes from plants. As plants grow, they need to take in nutrients from soil. Soil scientists figure out ways to make soil better for growing plants. Some of our food, such as milk, eggs, and meat, comes from farm animals.

CORN GROWING IN A FIELD

What are your three favorite foods?

NATURE'S NEIGHBORHOODS

Picture a pond on the edge of a grassy meadow. A bird swoops down over the water and catches an insect in its beak. Fish dart toward the shelter of some underwater plants. A deer wanders up to get a drink and stops to nibble on the leaves of a bush. Everything in this picture is part of an ecosystem—a kind of natural neighborhood.

An ecosystem can be a coral reef, a forest, or just what is underneath a log. An ecosystem includes all the plants and animals that live there, as well as the water, sunshine, air, and soil. Everything in an ecosystem depends on everything else in some way.

FACTS

ECOSYSTEM
a community of living things interacting with each other and their environment

ECOLOGY
(ih-KAH-luh-jee) the science of ecosystems

ECOLOGIST
a scientist who studies ecosystems

An **ECOLOGIST** observes how all the different parts of an **ECOSYSTEM** work together. The more we **UNDERSTAND** about an ecosystem, the more we can do to keep everything in it **HEALTHY**.

LIFE SCIENCE

BARN SWALLOW

SMALLMOUTH BASS

DEER

Ecologists explore different types of ecosystems all around the world. Here are just a few.

A **TROPICAL RAIN FOREST** is warm, wet, and green. Many kinds of plants and animals **LIVE TOGETHER** in this type of **ECOSYSTEM.**

A **DESERT** is dry. It can be hard to find any **LIVING THINGS** here at all. The animals and plants that live here must be able to **SURVIVE** with **VERY LITTLE WATER.**

MEERKATS

LIFE SCIENCE

A **GRASSLAND** is wide-open land, covered in **WAVING GRASS**. The animals that live here, such as **BISON AND ANTELOPE**, must always have plenty of grass **TO EAT.**

Which ecosystem would you most like to visit? Why?

A **TUNDRA** is dry, with winters that are **LONG AND COLD.** Here, plants stay small and grow **CLOSE TO THE GROUND.** Only the toughest cold-loving animals can **SURVIVE** in a tundra.

EXPLORING YOUR NEIGHBORHOOD

Your own backyard or neighborhood park is an ecosystem. Next time you go outside, try exploring that ecosystem like a scientist would.

LIFE SCIENCE

Try standing very still for a little while, and see what **ANIMALS** move around you. They might be on the **GROUND**, in the **SKY**, or in a **TREE**.

See if you can find out how many different plants and animals live in your own ecosystem. Make two columns on one of your science journal pages. Label one column "Plants" and one column "Animals." Then, whenever you go outside to play, take a moment to write down or draw a picture of every living thing you observe.

CHAPTER 3
EARTH AND SPACE

Earth scientists study the air, water, and rocks of our home planet. Space scientists study stars and other planets. Read about these scientists in this chapter.

PLANET EARTH

We all live on a planet called Earth. This planet is our home. Earth gives us air to breathe and water to drink. It gives us rocks for building things and soil for growing plants. All of us depend on Earth for our lives.

Astronauts in space take many pictures of Earth. The oceans make our planet look mostly blue. White clouds swirl through the sky. The rocks and soil of the land are gray and brown. Plants make parts of Earth look green.

FACTS

EARTH SCIENCE
the science of Earth

EARTH SCIENTIST
a scientist who studies planet Earth

EARTH
our planet, made up of air, water, soil, and rocks

ASTRONAUT

EARTH AND SPACE

EARTH

A **PLANETARY** scientist studies planets, including **EARTH,** and other objects in **SPACE.**

ROCKY WORLD

Next time you go outdoors, look closely at the ground. See if you can find a few small rocks. Along with soil, rocks make up most of the land under your feet.

ROCK HAMMER

GEOLOGISTS use **ROCK HAMMERS** to crack rocks open so they can **SEE INSIDE,** and to break off **SMALL PIECES** to study later.

Geologists look at the surface of Earth. They look deep inside Earth, too. They explore canyons, where they can see layers of rock stacked up like the layers of a birthday cake. Each layer can give geologists clues about what was going on at different times in Earth's past.

FACTS

GEOLOGY (jee-AH-luh-jee) the science of rocks

GEOLOGIST a scientist who studies rocks

EARTH AND SPACE

Finding, collecting, and sorting different kinds of rocks is fun. You can sort the rocks you find by color. Or you can feel the rocks with your fingertips and separate the rough rocks from the smooth ones. Or you might try lining them all up—from the largest to the smallest.

A geologist can tell you how, when, and where different kinds of rocks formed.

SANDSTONE

MUDSTONE

LIMESTONE

TRY THIS!

Can you find four things that are made of rock?

ANSWERS: castle, footpath, wall, statue

DIGGING UP THE PAST

A paleontologist examines a whale fossil in Egypt.

Looking for fossils is a lot like being on a treasure hunt. Paleontologists need a few hints before they know where to begin. Geologists make maps that show paleontologists where to find the rock layers that are most likely to hold fossils.

FACTS

FOSSIL
part of a living thing that has been preserved, or saved, in rock

PALEONTOLOGY
(pay-lee-ahn-TAH-luh-jee) the science of fossils

PALEONTOLOGIST
a scientist who studies fossils

DUCK-BILLED DINOSAUR

EARTH AND SPACE

In deep canyons, rock layers are exposed. Like geologists, paleontologists often look in areas like these. They scan for small pieces of fossil bone on the ground. Sometimes a trail of little pieces will lead right to a treasure. It may be a huge dinosaur bone, poking out of the rock in the canyon wall.

Paleontologists explore **ROCKS** and **ROCK LAYERS**, looking for **CLUES** about the life of the **PAST**.

Usually only part of the bone is showing. Most of it is still hidden in the rock. The scientists wonder what type of dinosaur it might be. Could it be a meat-eating tyrannosaur? Could it be a plant-eating duck-billed dinosaur? The only way to find out is to start digging!

SHELLS, LEAVES, and even **FOOTPRINTS** can be preserved as **FOSSILS**.

Paleontologists dig with picks and shovels. They fill buckets with rocks and soil and haul them away. As they dig, they uncover more bone fossils.

As they get close to the bones, the paleontologists begin using small tools such as awls, dental picks, and soft brushes to push away the soil and rock. They work slowly and carefully so they don't break any fossils.

They take pictures of the bones and make notes in their field journals. The data they collect will give them clues about how this dinosaur lived and died.

Once the fossils are out of the ground, the scientists take them to a museum. There they put the skeleton on display for all to see.

TYRANNOSAUR

AWL

VOLCANOES

Deep inside Earth—much deeper than where fossils are found—some of the rock gets very hot. In certain areas, there are pockets of hot, partly melted rock called magma. The magma pushes up through cracks in Earth's crust, or outer layer. Then, *boom!* It explodes out to the surface. Hot gases and ash shoot into the air. Hot melted rock pours out over the land. A volcano has erupted.

Volcano erupting in Ecuador

FACTS

VOLCANOLOGY (VAHL-kuh-NAH-luh-jee) the science of volcanoes—a branch of geology

VOLCANOLOGIST an earth scientist who studies volcanoes

EARTH AND SPACE

Scientists studying a volcano in Italy

Volcanologists use seismometers to record the rumblings inside volcanoes. Certain kinds of vibrations, or waves, mean that a volcano may erupt soon. Volcanologists warn people who live nearby so they have time to get to safety.

Underground, hot melted rock is called **MAGMA**. When it flows out of a **VOLCANO**, it is called **LAVA**.

VOLCANO

MAGMA

LAVA

EARTHQUAKE POWER

RESCUE WORKERS help people near a building that fell over during a large **EARTHQUAKE** in Taiwan.

FACTS

SEISMOLOGY
(size-MOL-uh-jee)
the science of earthquakes—a branch of geology

SEISMOLOGIST
a geologist who studies earthquakes

EARTH AND SPACE

In an earthquake, large sections of rock in Earth's crust slip suddenly. In buildings near the earthquake, walls rattle and shake. Pots and pans fall off their shelves. With most earthquakes, the shaking lasts for a moment or two, and then it stops.

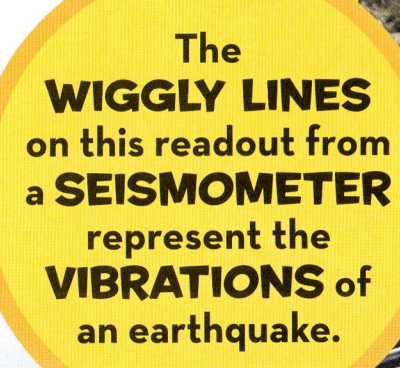

The **WIGGLY LINES** on this readout from a **SEISMOMETER** represent the **VIBRATIONS** of an earthquake.

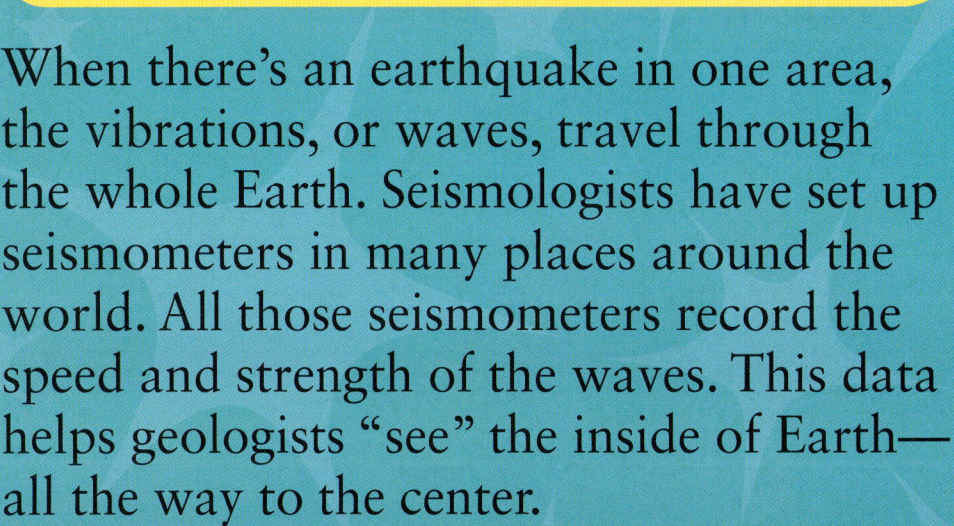

When there's an earthquake in one area, the vibrations, or waves, travel through the whole Earth. Seismologists have set up seismometers in many places around the world. All those seismometers record the speed and strength of the waves. This data helps geologists "see" the inside of Earth—all the way to the center.

DEEP BLUE OCEAN

FACTS

OCEANOGRAPHY (oh-shuh-NAH-gruh-fee) the science of oceans

OCEANOGRAPHER a scientist who studies the ocean

Oceanographers wonder what mysteries lie under the ocean's waves. To explore underwater, they wear diving gear and swim. Swim goggles help them get a good look.

Oceanographers at work in the Arctic

AIR TANK

WET SUIT

OCEANS cover nearly three-quarters of EARTH'S SURFACE.

EARTH AND SPACE

These scientists test the water to make sure it's healthy for all the plants and animals that live there. They take notes about the ocean bottom and all the creatures that make that area their home.

Over many months or years, oceanographers come back to the same area and record any changes. The data they collect helps scientists figure out ways to keep different ocean ecosystems healthy.

CORAL REEFS like this one are HOME to many kinds of FISH and OTHER ANIMALS.

SUBMERSIBLE

The deepest part of the ocean is in the **MARIANA TRENCH.** The place is called the **CHALLENGER DEEP.** You would have to travel nearly seven miles (11 km) **STRAIGHT DOWN** to get to the bottom of it!

Some parts of the ocean are way too deep for anyone to swim in, even with diving gear. In those areas, scientists need a submersible—a small, hard-sided vehicle that can dive down deep. It has its own power and an air supply for passengers.

Riding in submersibles, oceanographers can explore parts of the ocean that are so far down sunlight cannot reach them. Powerful lights help the scientists see what is there.

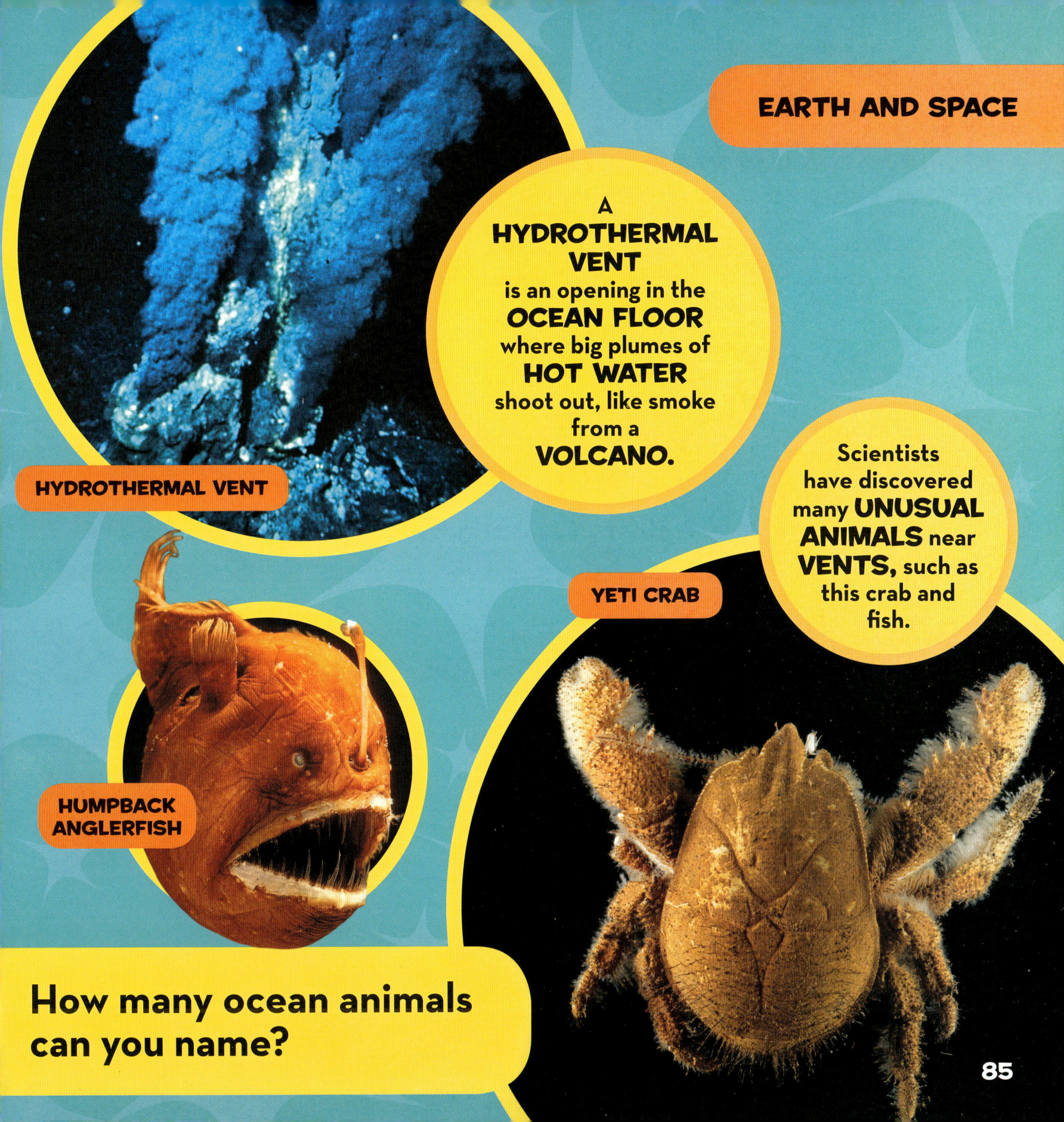

EARTH AND SPACE

A **HYDROTHERMAL VENT** is an opening in the **OCEAN FLOOR** where big plumes of **HOT WATER** shoot out, like smoke from a **VOLCANO.**

HYDROTHERMAL VENT

Scientists have discovered many **UNUSUAL ANIMALS** near **VENTS,** such as this crab and fish.

YETI CRAB

HUMPBACK ANGLERFISH

How many ocean animals can you name?

85

WATCHING THE WEATHER

While oceanographers search the ocean, meteorologists keep their eyes on the sky. Meteorologists keep track of the weather every day. They measure the temperature of the air. They measure the air pressure and how fast the wind is blowing. Meteorologists use all the data they collect to try to figure out what the weather will be.

FACTS

METEOROLOGY (MEE-tee-uh-RAHL-uh-jee) the science of the air and the weather

METEOROLOGIST a scientist who studies the air and figures out what the weather will be

A **THERMOMETER** measures how **HOT OR COLD** something is.

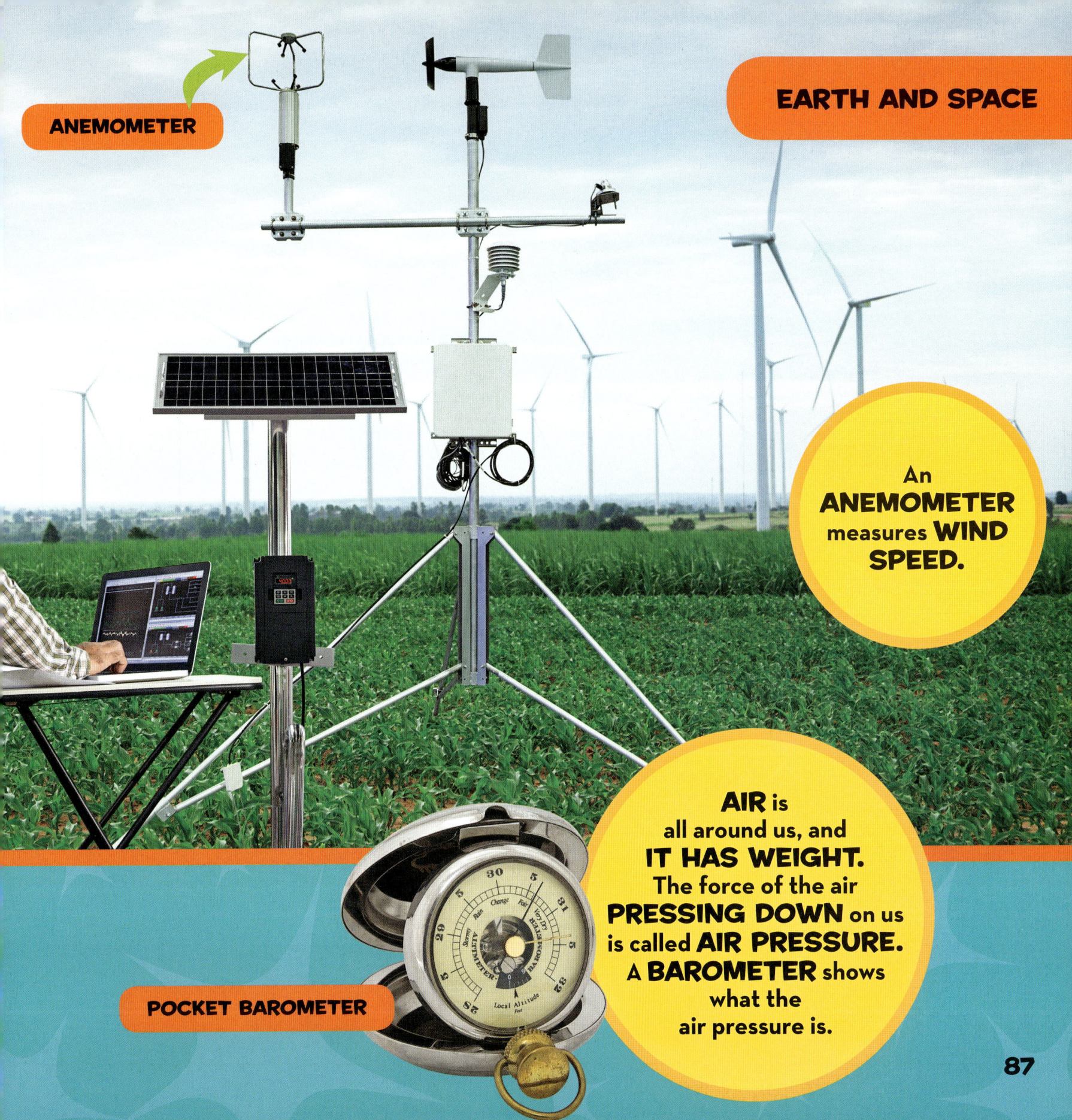

ANEMOMETER

EARTH AND SPACE

An **ANEMOMETER** measures **WIND SPEED.**

POCKET BAROMETER

AIR is all around us, and **IT HAS WEIGHT.** The force of the air **PRESSING DOWN** on us is called **AIR PRESSURE.** A **BAROMETER** shows what the air pressure is.

Meteorologists keep an eye on dangerous storms. These scientists warn people ahead of time when a storm is coming so everyone can stay safe.

A CLOUD is made up of tiny **WATER** droplets. It takes about **A MILLION DROPLETS** to make **ONE RAINDROP** that is heavy enough to fall.

WEATHER RADAR TRUCK

SCIENTISTS TRACKING A BIG STORM

What is your favorite type of weather?

TRY THIS!
Keep a Weather Journal

When you see dark clouds in the sky, you can probably predict that it will rain soon. Keeping a weather journal will help you become even better at telling what the weather will be.

In your journal, make a chart with spaces for every day of the month. At the end of each day, mark down if it was sunny, cloudy, rainy, snowy, or windy. Some days may have two or more kinds of weather. Be sure to record it all.

Try to keep track of the weather every day for at least a month. Here's an example of what a weather journal might look like.

RISING TEMPERATURES

Climate scientists look at huge amounts of weather data, recorded over many years. They compare the data from year to year. That helps them spot changes that might be happening.

Today, change is happening very quickly in the Arctic region. Climate scientists travel there many times each year. They measure the air temperature. They take photos of glaciers, and they measure the glaciers' size.

The studies show that temperatures are going up. Glaciers are melting and shrinking. All the data climate scientists gather will help them figure out why Earth's overall climate is changing and how fast.

FACTS

CLIMATE (KLEYE-muht) the usual weather of an area over a long period of time—at least 30 years

CLIMATE SCIENTIST a scientist who studies Earth's climate

EARTH AND SPACE

GLACIERS are vast, thick fields of **ICE.** They form in **COLD AREAS** where many **LAYERS OF SNOW** build up over **HUNDREDS OF YEARS.**

These scientists are taking pictures inside a **GLACIER. WATER MELTING** off the glacier's surface made this **TUNNEL** in the ice.

Scientist at a glacier in Alaska

OUTER SPACE

The sun goes down, and you look up into the dark night sky. You see stars twinkling in the blackness. When you look at the stars, you're seeing all the way into outer space. Stars are far, far away. Giant telescopes help astronomers observe the stars more closely. Our own sun is a star. It's the star closest to Earth. Astronomers study the differences between our sun and other stars.

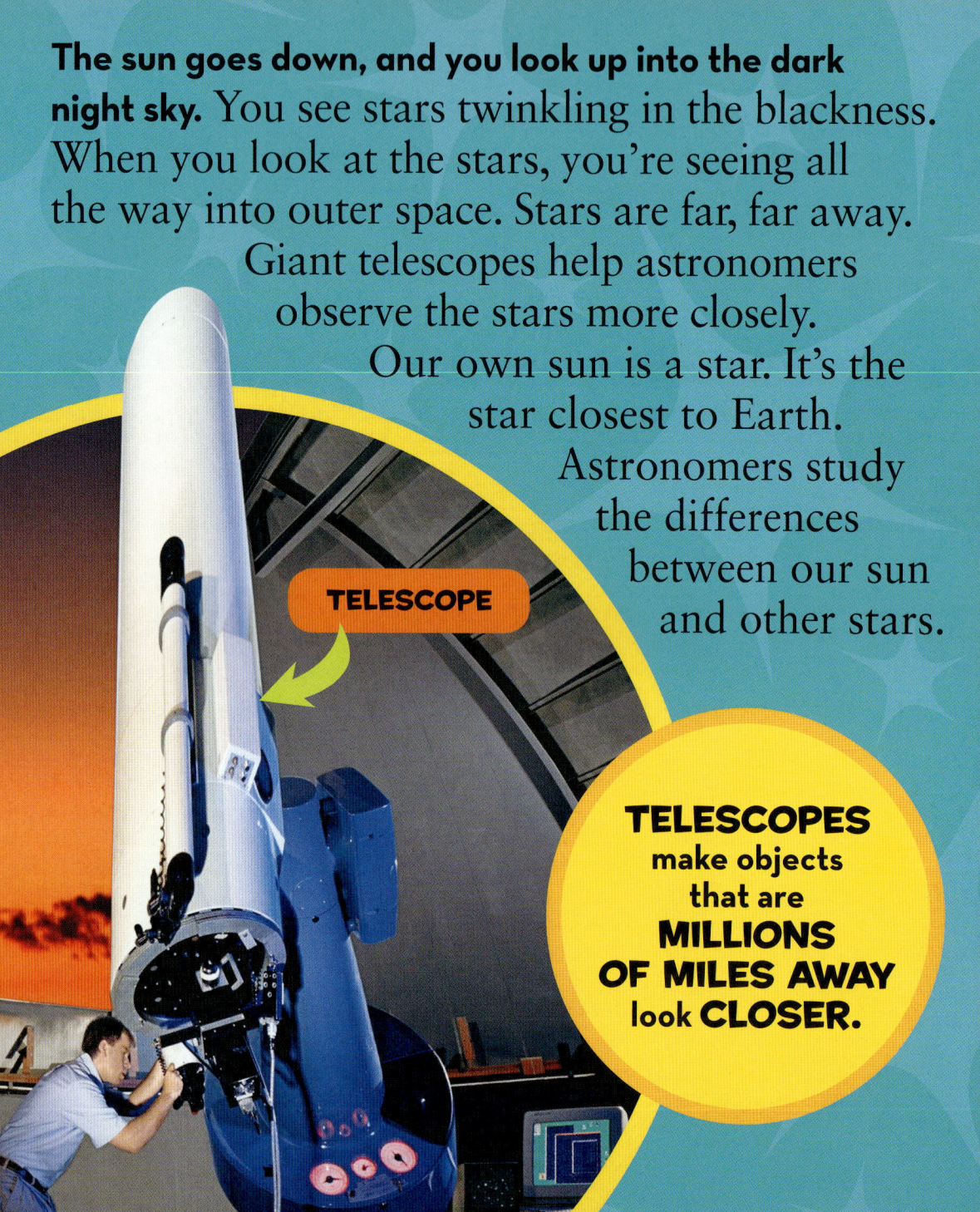

TELESCOPE

TELESCOPES make objects that are **MILLIONS OF MILES AWAY** look **CLOSER.**

EARTH AND SPACE

Our **SUN** is one among **BILLIONS OF STARS** that make up our home galaxy—**THE MILKY WAY.**

FACTS

ASTRONOMY
(uh-STRAH-nuh-mee)
the science of stars and planets

ASTRONOMER
a scientist who studies stars and planets

Astronomers also study Earth's moon and the other planets that orbit our sun. The moon is the only place in space where people have landed.

Someday astronauts may visit other planets. For now, scientists send remote-controlled robots called space probes to explore. Probes have landed on Mars and Venus. They have flown close to other planets.

Space probes collect data and take pictures and send them back to scientists on Earth. They help us learn more about what the planets are made of and search for signs of life.

Twelve **ASTRONAUTS** have walked **ON THE MOON.** They brought some moon **ROCKS** back to Earth **FOR SCIENTISTS TO STUDY.**

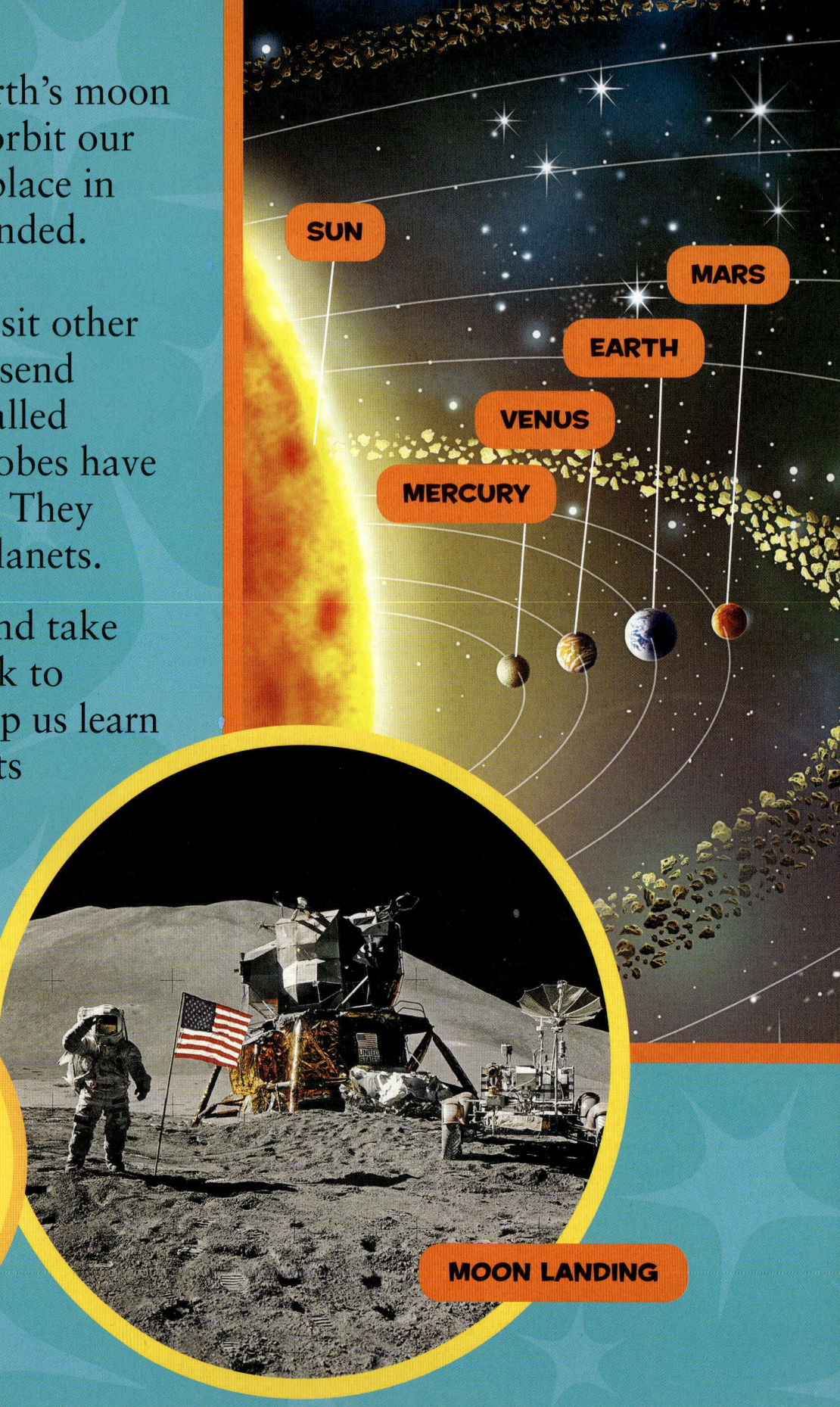

SUN
MERCURY
VENUS
EARTH
MARS

MOON LANDING

CHAPTER 4
PHYSICAL SCIENCE

This chapter introduces you to the work of physical scientists, who discover what things are made of and how things move and change.

EVERYTHING IS MATTER

As you look around, you see a lot of familiar things. Your house, toys, pets, food, rocks, soil, water, air—all the stuff around you is called matter. Matter is anything that can be weighed or measured and that takes up space—including you!

FACTS

MATTER
everything in the world is made of matter

PHYSICAL SCIENCE
everything about matter, including how it moves and changes

PHYSICAL SCIENCE

Long ago, scientists discovered that all matter is made up of tiny particles called atoms. There are about 115 different types of atoms. They are way too small for anyone to see, but you can think of them as 115 different shapes of building blocks. Atoms can fit together in millions of different ways. Everything in the world is made from those tiny building blocks.

Two or more **ATOMS** often **STICK TOGETHER** to form a different kind of **PARTICLE** called a **MOLECULE**.

A **LABORATORY** is a room or building filled with **THE TOOLS** chemists need.

SAFETY GOGGLES

FLASK

BEAKER

MICROSCOPE

MIX AND STIR

A chemist studies how matter changes. By mixing substances and measuring carefully along the way, chemists hope to make new or different substances that people can use.

FACTS

CHEMISTRY (KEH-muh-stree) the science of how matter changes

CHEMIST a scientist who studies chemistry

PHYSICAL SCIENCE

If you mix two substances in a beaker—for example, baking soda and vinegar—you are doing chemistry. Baking soda and vinegar by themselves are not too exciting. But when they are mixed together, watch out! A chemical reaction takes place. The reaction creates a new substance—a gas called carbon dioxide—that makes bubbles overflow the beaker.

TEST TUBE

CHEMISTS mix substances in **GLASS BEAKERS,** cylinders, and **TEST TUBES.**

CARBON DIOXIDE is the gas that makes soda drinks **FIZZY.**

Sometimes substances can be mixed without a chemical reaction happening. Lemonade is made up of three substances: water, lemon juice, and sugar. When you stir sugar into water and lemon juice, the sugar dissolves. The molecules of sugar spread out through the liquid, but they don't turn into something different. There are still three kinds of molecules in your glass: water, lemon juice, and sugar. But you have changed the lemonade—now it's sweeter!

Heating and cooling are other ways chemists can make substances change. You can try it, too. Pour some of your lemonade into an ice cube tray, put it into the freezer, and wait about an hour.

PHYSICAL SCIENCE

ICE

When the lemonade gets cold enough, it will change from a liquid to a solid. Let the solid lemonade cubes warm up for a while, and you will see them turn back into liquid.

There are **THREE STATES** of matter: **SOLID, LIQUID,** and **GAS. ICE** is the solid state of water.

When a **LIQUID** gets hot enough, it **CHANGES ITS STATE** to become a **GAS.** Boiling water creates steam—water as a **GAS.**

STEAM

What do you like to drink on a hot day?

MOVING FORCES

FACTS

PHYSICS (FIZZ-icks) the science of how matter moves and the forces that make things move

PHYSICIST a scientist who studies physics

PHYSICAL SCIENCE

When you are not playing with your toy car or truck, it just sits there doing nothing. What happens if you give it a push? *Zoom!* Off it goes. You can also pull your car with a string to make it go. Physicists call pushes and pulls forces. Forces make things move.

Another type of force is gravity. Gravity is always pulling everything—including you—down toward the center of Earth. Gravity makes things fall down. When you jump up, you always come back down because the force of gravity pulls you toward the ground.

What are some of your favorite ways to move?

WAVES OF SOUND

When you toss a rock into a pond, the water moves away from the rock in waves. What happens when you drop a metal spoon over a hard floor? Try it. The spoon falls down, hits the floor, and makes a big sound. *Clank!*

When the spoon lands on the floor, it makes the floor vibrate. The vibrations move through the air in the same way waves move through water in a pond. These vibrations are called sound waves. When they reach your ears, you hear the sound of the spoon hitting the floor.

When you speak or sing, the **VOCAL CORDS** in your throat **VIBRATE.** The vibrations move out **THROUGH THE AIR IN WAVES.**

TRY THIS!

Hold a drumstick in one hand and put your fingertips on the side of a drum. Bang the drum with the stick. You can hear the tap of your drumstick. Can you feel it, too? You are feeling the sound waves. Try putting a few grains of sand or cornmeal on the drum and see if you can see the sound as well.

WAVES OF LIGHT

PHYSICISTS study how light moves. **LIGHT TRAVELS IN WAVES** that can go through **AIR** and **SPACE.**

Look around your bedroom. Turn off all the lights. Pull down the shades or close the curtains so that no sunlight gets in. Suddenly your room looks different. It may seem like all the color has drained out of things. That's because you need light to help you see color.

PHYSICAL SCIENCE

PRISM

A PRISM bends a **BEAM OF LIGHT.** As the light beam bends, all the different **COLORS IN THE LIGHT** get **SEPARATED.**

All waves— **SOUND** waves, **LIGHT** waves, **OCEAN** waves— **CARRY ENERGY** from one place to another.

Light is made up of seven colors: red, orange, yellow, green, blue, indigo, and violet. Light bounces off every object it strikes. When you look at a leaf, you see that it is green. That means most of the light bouncing off the leaf is green light. As soon as your eyes see that light, you know the color of the leaf.

IT'S SHOCKING!

If you put on a pair of wool socks, shuffle across a carpet, and then touch a metal doorknob—*zap!* You feel a little shock. You may even see a quick spark of light jump between your finger and the knob.

Long ago, physicists wondered about this strange force. They named it static electricity. The electricity that powers our homes is called current electricity.

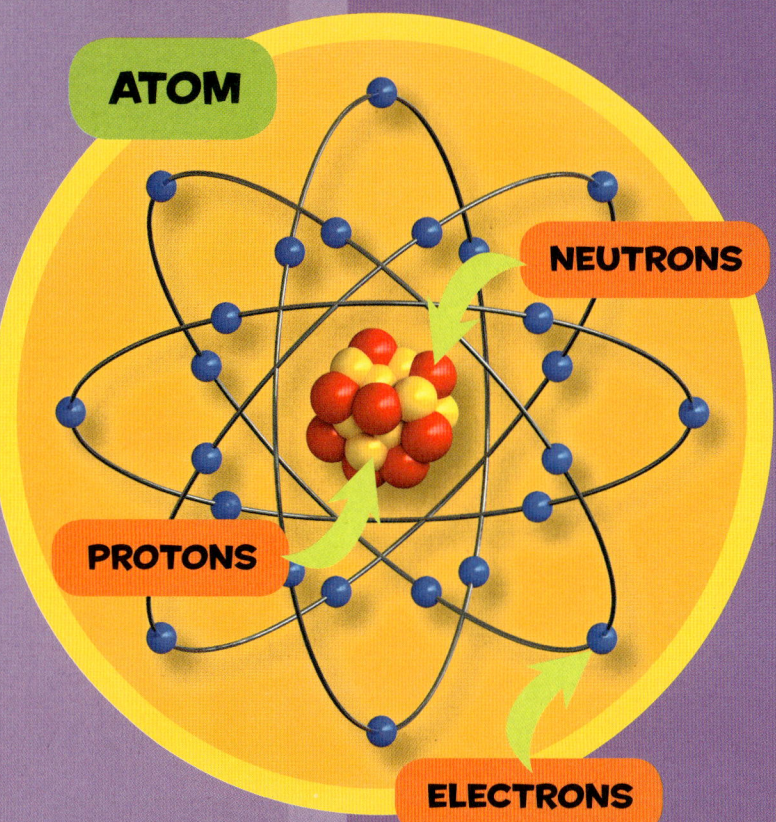

ATOM
NEUTRONS
PROTONS
ELECTRONS

PHYSICAL SCIENCE

Electricity flows through wires from a big power plant to the electrical outlets in your house. It flows from an outlet through the wire to your lamp. The lightbulb changes the electricity into light.

Atoms, the tiny particles that make up all matter, are made up of even tinier particles called protons, neutrons, and electrons. Electrons are always moving. In static electricity, electrons jump from one object to another. In current electricity, electrons flow in one direction through a wire.

Before **SCIENTISTS** figured out how to use **ELECTRICITY** to make light, people read by the **LIGHT** of a **CANDLE** or **OIL LAMP** at night.

TRY THIS!

You use electricity every day to turn on the lights and to make other devices work. How many of the objects here need electricity to make them work?

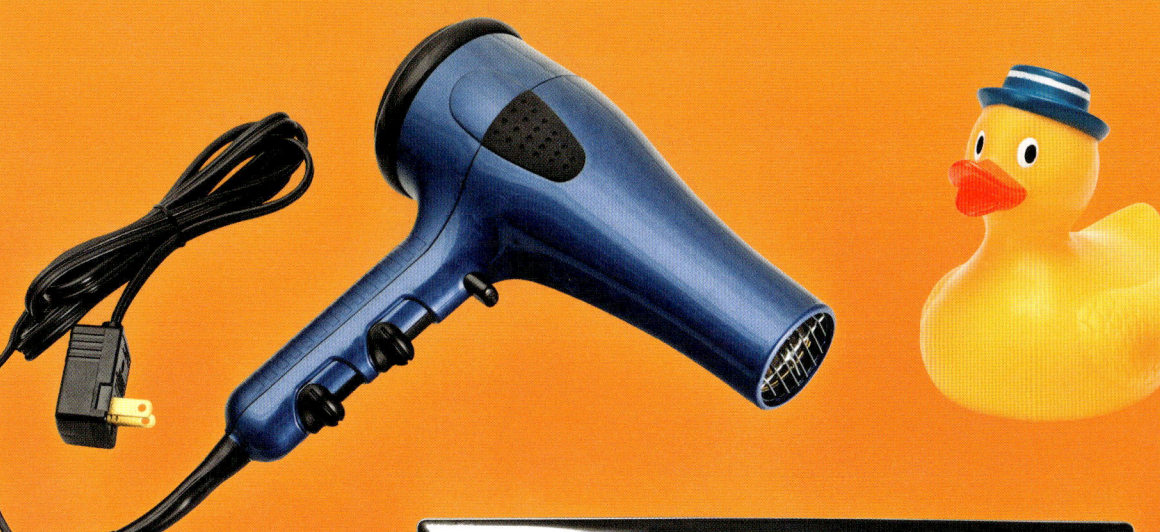

ANSWER: Seven—microwave, cell phone, vacuum, hair dryer, TV, lamp, toaster

113

CHAPTER 5
GREAT INVENTIONS

Scientific knowledge helps engineers design and build new things. In this chapter, you will see some of the world's greatest inventions—brought to us by engineers.

TRY, TRY AGAIN

Engineers use scientific knowledge to invent new things and to improve things that are already invented. Thanks to engineers, we have phones and cars, bikes and bridges. We have lights and clocks, boats and refrigerators.

WINGS

A glider, an early flying machine

Great inventions like the airplane don't happen all at once. Long ago, inventors watched birds flying. They strapped feathered wings to their arms and tried flying like birds themselves. When that didn't work, other inventors tried building flying machines.

FACTS

ENGINEERING (en-jin-EER-ing) the use of scientific knowledge to solve problems

ENGINEER someone who thinks about problems, and designs and builds useful new things to solve those problems

GREAT GRAY OWL

GREAT INVENTIONS

Over time, inventors realized that the shape of the wings was the key to flying. Finally, those early flying machines started to work. They glided through the air for short distances. Eventually, engineers figured out how to build engines to power airplanes so they could stay up in the air longer, fly faster, and travel farther.

Computers and smartphones were **DESIGNED** by **ENGINEERS.**

TYPES OF ENGINEERS

Different kinds of engineers use knowledge from different branches of science. Here are descriptions of some of the work they do.

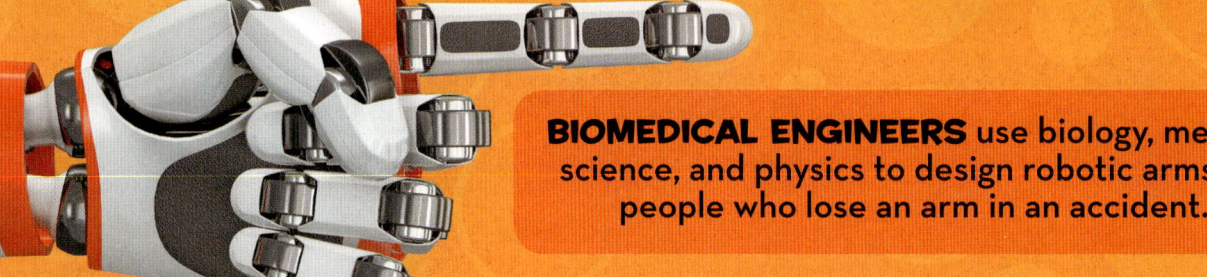

BIOMEDICAL ENGINEERS use biology, medical science, and physics to design robotic arms for people who lose an arm in an accident.

AEROSPACE ENGINEERS use astronomy and physics to design spacecraft that will make it possible for humans to fly to other planets.

MECHANICAL ENGINEERS use physics to design a robotic car that can drive itself.

GREAT INVENTIONS

ENVIRONMENTAL ENGINEERS work to keep ecosystems healthy and clean.

ELECTRICAL ENGINEERS design solar panels that use energy from the sun to generate electricity.

One thing every engineer and scientist knows is that science is never finished. As soon as you discover an answer to one of your big questions, it will lead to many more questions. As soon as you come up with a good design, you'll be thinking of ways to make it better. In science, there is always more to explore and more to invent!

What would you like to invent?

PROBLEM-SOLVING

An engineer works step-by-step, just like a scientist does. You can add an engineering section to your science journal. Fill it with all your great engineering ideas. You can draw pictures of your designs and show others how they work.

Some designs don't work very well. Those can be set aside, and new ideas can be tried. Keep experimenting!

Science Journal

My Problem: My cars just sit there when I'm not pushing them. Boring!

My Question: How can I use the force of gravity to make my cars go?

My Hypothesis: When I go down the slide, I go fast because gravity pulls me. I could make a slide for my cars.

What I Made: I cut two pieces of sturdy cardboard. I made sure they were the same size by measuring them. Each one was three feet (1 m) long and one foot (30 cm) wide. These were my slides.

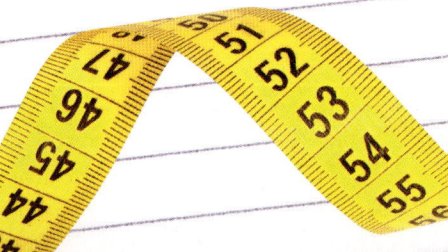

GREAT INVENTIONS

How I Tested My Design:
1. I set the slides side by side.
2. I put one thick book under the end of one and two thick books under the other.
3. I held one car at the top of each slide. I let go of them at the same time.

How It Worked: The car on the slide with two books went faster and farther than the other car.

What I Learned: The higher the slide, the faster the car goes.

More Questions: What if I put three books under one slide? Is higher always better? Is there such a thing as a slide that is too high?

Ideas for Making My Design Better: Sometimes one of my cars falls off the side of my slide. Maybe if my slides had sides, my car races would go better.

Have **FUN** and be **CREATIVE**. When you use your **IMAGINATION** and **KNOWLEDGE** of science, amazing things can happen!

PARENT TIPS

Extend your child's experience beyond the pages of this book. A visit to a science museum is one way to get children interested in different aspects of science. Your local library is a good source for books of hands-on science experiments and activities that are age-appropriate for your child. Here are a few ideas to get you started.

SHADOW PLAY (PHYSICS)

All you need is a flashlight and a blank wall. Shine the beam of light at the wall and have your child put a hand in front of the beam. Invite him to observe the shadow made by his hand. Let him know that he is actually blocking a beam of light. See how many shadow shapes he can make. Ask him if he can make the shape of a bird. Then encourage him to experiment. Can he make a rabbit? A dog? A crocodile?

SOLID OR LIQUID? (CHEMISTRY)

If you have a box of cornstarch at home, you and your child can mix up some oobleck. Oobleck is humorously named for the gooey stuff in a Dr. Seuss book. Put 1 cup (250 mL) of water in a large bowl. Slowly sprinkle in 2 cups (220 g) of cornstarch, stirring as you go. Keep mixing until it feels smooth and gooey.

Have your child describe this amazing new substance. Does she think it is a liquid or a solid? Have her try to pour it from one bowl into another. She can poke it and tap it. Roll some of it into a ball in your hands. Stop and let the ball sit on your palm for a moment. Ask your child to describe what happens.

Oobleck sometimes acts like a liquid and sometimes like a solid. If your child loves new science words you can tell her that oobleck is a "non-Newtonian fluid."

EGG, PLUS HEAT (CHEMISTRY)

Chemistry is all about change, and one way we change substances every day is through cooking. Heating up a frying pan together can be a good time to talk with your child about safety around the stove. Have your child crack a raw egg and slide it gently into the pan. Encourage him to watch the egg as it cooks. See if he can describe all the changes that happen as the egg heats up. Does it begin to look, sound, and smell different?

NATURE WALK (ECOLOGY)

There's nothing quite as satisfying as a nature walk to get kids thinking like scientists. Whenever you take a walk together in your local park or nature center, encourage observations and questions. You can turn this fun activity into a genuine scientific endeavor by helping your child start a nature journal, in which she can draw and write about her observations and share them with others.

MOON SHAPES (ASTRONOMY)

With the right opportunity, many children love gazing up at the night sky. If you live in an area where it's easy to get outdoors, you can choose a few evenings for observing the moon. (Consult a lunar calendar to know when the moon will rise and what phase it will be in on any given evening.)

Ask your child to draw the shape of the moon each night. If your child becomes curious about why the moon is changing, you can look for a book together at your local library. A pair of binoculars or a telescope will give your child a good view of the moon's craters.

HOUSE OF BLOCKS (ENGINEERING)

A set of toy blocks is a great tool for your child to experiment with physical forces and to figure out how to design and build more and more complex, but stable, structures.

SCIENCE IS ALL AROUND US

You don't have to set up special activities to do science with your children. All you need is to encourage their questions. Then, give them space and time to come up with their own hypotheses, or predictions. When they want assistance, help them become better observers by pointing out details they may not have noticed at first. Help them learn to weigh and measure things as accurately as possible. Challenge them to compare and contrast the different quantities and qualities of things, and assist them in their quest to find answers at the library or online.

GLOSSARY

ABDOMEN: the hind part of an insect's body; the belly of a mammal

ARCTIC: the northernmost part of the world, around the North Pole

ASTRONAUT: a person who is specially trained to travel in outer space

ATOM: the smallest particle of matter that still has the same qualities and behaviors of the substance it came from; atoms are made up of neutrons, protons, and electrons

CHRYSALIS: the protective covering of a pupa as it develops into a butterfly

CLIMATE: an area's normal weather, measured over a long period of time—usually 30 years or more

COMPUTER: a machine that can store and recall huge amounts of data, make lightning-fast calculations, and spot patterns in data

DISSOLVE: to mix a solid substance or a gas into a liquid substance

ELECTRICITY: a form of energy caused by the flow of electrons

ELECTRON: the smallest part of an atom; electrons move around the center of an atom

ENERGY: the ability to move or to do work

GAS: one of the three main states of matter

GERMS: tiny, one-celled living things that can infect a person or animal and make them sick

HEAT: to add energy to a substance, raising its temperature

LIFE CYCLE: the series of changes that a living thing goes through as it is born, grows to adulthood, has its young, gets older, and dies

LIQUID: one of the three main states of matter

MOLECULE: two or more atoms linked together by a chemical bond

NEUTRONS: tiny particles that, together with protons, make up the center of atoms

NUTRIENT: an ingredient in food for people, animals, or plants that helps growth and good health

OUTER SPACE: the universe beyond Earth's atmosphere

OXYGEN: a gas in the air and dissolved in water

PLANET: a large, round object that orbits a star

PREDATOR: an animal that hunts for and eats other animals

PREDICT: to use observations and evidence to tell what is going to happen

PROTONS: tiny particles that, together with neutrons, make up the center of atoms

RAIN FOREST: a dense woodland in an area that gets a lot of rain

REEF: a ridge of rock or coral in a shallow part of the ocean

SKELETON: the bones inside the bodies of all vertebrates—fish, amphibians, reptiles, birds, and mammals

SMARTPHONE: a cell phone with a built-in computer

SOLAR SYSTEM: a star and the objects that orbit it

SOLID: one of the three main states of matter

STAR: a large, bright, round object in space made up of hot, glowing gases, such as the sun

SUBSTANCE: the matter from which any particular thing is made

THORAX: the middle part of an insect's body

VIBRATE: to move back and forth or up and down very rapidly

VIRUS: an extremely tiny, nonliving infectious particle that can make a person or animal sick

VOCAL CORDS: the pair of bands in your throat that vibrate when you move your breath past them, producing the sound of your voice

WAVE: a vibrating motion; sound waves move through air, water, or solids; light waves travel through empty space

WEATHER: the combined temperature, wind, and water in the air at any particular time and place

ADDITIONAL RESOURCES

Boyer, Crispin. *National Geographic Kids Why?: Over 1,111 Answers to Everything.* National Geographic Kids Books, 2015.

Boyer, Crispin. *National Geographic Kids Why Not?: Over 1,111 Answers to Everything.* National Geographic Kids Books, 2018.

Esbaum, Jill. *Little Kids First Big Book of How.* National Geographic Kids Books, 2016.

Esbaum, Jill. *Little Kids First Big Book of Why 2.* National Geographic Kids Books, 2018.

Science Encyclopedia: Atom Smashing, Food Chemistry, Animals, Space, and More! National Geographic Kids Books, 2016.

Shields, Amy. *Little Kids First Big Book of Why.* National Geographic Kids Books, 2011.

INDEX

Boldface indicates illustrations. If illustrations are included within a page span, the entire span is **boldface**.

A
Abdomen **37**, 124
Aerospace engineering 118, **118**
Agriculture 58-59, **58-59**
Air pressure 87
Airplanes and flying machines **114-117**
Amphibians **44-46**
Anemometers 87, **87**
Anglerfish **85**
Animals
 all about animals 34-35, **34-35**
 amphibians **44-46**
 birds **35, 48-51**, 61, **116-117**
 branches of science 22-23, **22-23**
 fish 42-43, **42-43**, 61, **85**
 insects **28, 29, 36-39**
 mammals **21, 26-27, 52-55**, 61
 reptiles 44, 46-47, **46-47**
 shelled animals 40-41, **40-41**
 spiders 38, **38**
 veterinarians 25, **25**
Ants 37, **37**
Arctic regions **82**, 90, 124
Astronauts **67**, 68, **68**, 94, **94**, 124
Astronomy **21**, 92-95, 123
Atoms 99, 111, **111**, 124

B
Backyard ecosystems 64-65, **64-65**
Barn swallows 61
Barometers 87, **87**
Beavers 55, **55**
Beetles **29, 38-39**
Binoculars 49, **49**
Biology see Life science
Biomedical engineers 118
Birds **35, 48-51**, 61, **116-117**
Birds of paradise 49, **49**
Black-naped blue flycatchers **50**
Bones 32-33, **32-33**
Botany 56-57, **56-57**
Branches of science 22-23, **22-23**
Butterflies **36, 36, 38-39**

C
Camels **93**
Carbon dioxide 101
Cars, robotic 118, **118**
Caterpillars **28**
Cats **53**
Challenger Deep 84
Chameleons **35**
Chemistry **20, 100-103**, 122
Chrysalises **36, 36**, 124
Cicadas **37**
Clams 41, **41**
Climate 90-91, **90-91**, 124
Colors, in light 109, **109**
Computers 124
Control (experiment part) 17
Coral reefs **83, 83**, 125
Corn **59**
Cows **58**
Crabs **85**
Crickets **38-39**
Crocodiles 46, **46-47**
Curiosity (space probe) 95, **95**
Current electricity 110-113

D
Data 15, 19
Deer **61**
Deserts 62, **62**
Dinosaurs **74-75**, 75-77
Discovery (space shuttle) 24, **24**
Dissolve, defined 124
Diving 82-83, **82-83**
Doctors **4**, 30-33
Dogs **52**, 72
Dragonflies **37, 38-39**
Drums 107, **107**
Duck-billed dinosaurs **75**

E
Earth **67-81**
 climate 90-91, **90-91**, 124
 earthquakes 80-81, **80-81**
 oceans **82-85**, 109, **109**
 paleontology **2-3, 74-77**
 planet Earth 68-69, **68-69**, 94-95, 95
 rocks **70-73**
 volcanoes **20-21**, 78-79, **78-79**
 weather **86-89**, 125
Earthquakes 80-81, **80-81**
Echidnas 53, **53**
Ecosystems **60-65**
 backyard 64-65, **64-65**
 defined 60
 environmental engineering 119, **119**
 oceans 83
 parent tips 123
 types of 62-63, **62-63**
Electrical engineers 119
Electricity **110-113**, 119, **119**, 124
Electrons 111, **111**, 124
Elephants **54**, 55, **55**
Emerald tree boas **46-47**, 47
Energy 124
Engineering **114-121**
 defined 116
 inventions **114-121**
 parent tips 123
 problem-solving 120-121, **120-121**
 types of 118-119, **118-119**
Entomology **36-39**
Environment see Ecosystems
Experiments **14-19**
 data 15, 19
 hypotheses 14, 18-19
 journal 16-17, **16-17**
 sharing what you learn 18-19, **18-19**
 theories 18

126

F
Farming 58-59, **58-59**
Field crickets **38-39**
Fish 42-43, **42-43**, 61, 85
Flowers 56, **56**
Flycatchers (birds) **50**
Flying lizards 47, **47**
Food, growing 58-59, **58-59**
Forces 104-105, **104-105**
Fossils 2-3, 74-77
Frogs 35, 45, **45**

G
Gases 103, **103**, 124
Geese 50, **50**
Gentoo penguins **49**
Geology 70-71, **70-71**
Germs 30, 124
Giraffes **35**, 55, **55**
Glaciers 90-91, **90-91**
Gliders 116, **116**
Glossary 124-125
Golden orb weaver spiders **38**
Gorillas 54, **54**
Grasslands 63, **63**
Gravity 105
Great gray owls **116-117**
Green darner dragonfly **38-39**
Green violet-ear hummingbirds **51**
Guinea pigs 15, **15**

H
Hearing, sense of 12, **12**
Heat 124
Herpetology **44-47**
Human body
   medicine **30-33**
   robotic arm 118, **118**
   senses 12-13, **12-13**
   vocal cords 107, 125
Hummingbirds **51**
Humpback anglerfish **85**
Humpback whales **29**
Hydrothermal vents 85, **85**
Hypotheses 14, 18-19

I
Ichthyology 42-43, **42-43**
Insects 28, 29, 36-39
Inventions **114-121**
   airplanes and flying machines **114-117**
   problem-solving 120-121, **120-121**
   types of engineers 118-119, **118-119**
Invertebrates 37

J
Journals
   experiments 16-17, **16-17**
   problem-solving 120-121, **120-121**
   weather 89, **89**
Jupiter (planet) **95**

K
King bird of paradise **49**
Koalas **4**

L
Laboratories 100, **100**
Lava 79, **79**
Lemonade **102**, 102-103
Life cycle 124

Life science (biology) **26-65**
   all living things 28-29, **28-29**
   amphibians **44-46**
   birds 35, 48-51, 61, 116-117
   branches of science 22-23, **22-23**
   ecosystems **60-65**, 83, 119, **119**, 123
   fish 42-43, **42-43**, 61, 85
   human body 12-13, **12-13**, 30-33, 107, 118, **118**, 125
   insects 28, 29, 36-39
   mammals 21, 26-27, 52-55, 61
   plants **56-59**, 75, **75**
   reptiles 44, 46-47, **46-47**
   shelled animals 40-41, **40-41**
Light waves 108-109, 125
Limestone **71**
Lions 55, **55**
Liquids 103, 122, 124
Lizards 46-47, **47**

M
Macaws **35**
Magma 78-79, **79**
Malacology 40-41, **40-41**
Mammals 21, 26-27, 52-55, 61
Mariana Trench 84, **84**
Mars (planet) 94, 95, **95**
Matter 98-99, **98-99**, 100, 103
Mechanical engineers 118
Medical science **30-33**, 118, **118**
Meerkats **62**
Mercury (planet) **94**
Meteorology 21, 86-89
Mice 29, 55, **55**
Microscopes 58-59
Migration 50
Milky Way 93, **93**
Molecules 99, 102, 124
Mollusks 40-41, **40-41**
Monarch butterflies **28**, 36, **36-37**
Moon 94, **94**, 123
Mountain gorillas 54, **54**
Moving forces 104-105, **104-105**
Mudstone **71**
Music 107, **107**

N
Neighborhood ecosystems 64-65, **64-65**
Neptune (planet) **95**
Neutrons 111, **111**, 124
Nile crocodiles 46, **46-47**
Nutrients 124

O
Observation 12-13, **12-13**
Ocean animals
   coral reefs 83, **83**, 125
   fish 42-43, **42-43**, 61, 85
   near hydrothermal vents 85, **85**
   shelled animals 40-41, **40-41**
Oceans **82-85**, 109, **109**
Octopuses 41, **41**
Oobleck 122
Ornithology **48-51**
Outer space see Space
Owls **116-117**
Oxygen 28, 124

P
Painted turtles **47**
Paleontology 2-3, **74-77**
Pandas 21, **35**

Parent tips 122-123, **122-123**
Penguins **49**
Physical science **96-113**
   atoms 99, 111, **111**, 124
   chemistry **20**, **100-103**, 122
   electricity **110-113**, 119, **119**, 124
   light waves 108-109, 125
   matter 98-99, **98-99**, 100, 103
   moving forces 104-105, **104-105**
   parent tips 122
   sound waves 106-107, 109, 125
   states of matter 102-103, 122
Planets 69, 94-95, **94-95**, 124
Plants **56-59**, 75, **75**
Platypuses 53, **53**
Predators 125
Predictions 125
Prisms 109, **109**
Problem-solving 120-121, **120-121**
Protons 111, **111**, 125

R
Rain forests 62, **62**, 125
Rainfall 88, **88**
Rays (fish) 43, **43**
Red-eyed tree frogs **35**
Reefs 83, **83**, 125
Reptiles 44, 46-47, **46-47**
Robins 48, **48**
Rocks **70-73**
Rovers (space probes) 95, **95**

S
Salamanders 44, **44**
Sandstone **71**
Saturn (planet) **95**
Scallops 41, **41**
Scarlet macaws **35**
Science, introduction to **8-25**
   asking questions 10-11, **10-11**
   branches of science 22-23, **22-23**
   experiments **14-19**
   hypotheses 14, 18-19
   kinds of scientists 20-21, **20-21**
   observation 12-13, **12-13**
   parent tips 123
   scientific knowledge 24-25, **24-25**
Seashells 40-41, **40-41**
Seeds 56-57
Seismology 79, 80-81, **80-81**
Senses 12-13, **12-13**
Shadow play 122
Sharks 43, **43**
Shelled animals 40-41, **40-41**
Sight, sense of 12, **12**
Silvery blue butterfly **38-39**
Skeleton **32-33**, 125
Smallmouth bass **61**
Smartphones 117, **117**, 125
Smell, sense of 13, **13**
Snakes 46-47, **46-47**
Snow geese 50, **50**
Soil 59, **59**
Solar panels 119, **119**
Solar system **94-95**, 125
Solids 103, **103**, 122, 125
Sound waves 106-107, 109, 125
Space
   astronauts 67, 68, **68**, 94, **94**, 124
   engineering 118, **118**
   outer space 21, **66-67**, **92-95**, 124
   parent tips 123

   space probes 94-95, **95**
   space shuttle 24, **24**
Spiders 38, **38**
Stars 92, **93**, 125
States of matter 102-103, 122
Static electricity 110-111
Stethoscopes 30, **30**
Stinkbugs **38-39**
Storms 88, **88**
Strawberries 59
Submersibles 84, **84**
Substances 125
Sun 94

T
Tadpoles 45, **45**
Taste, sense of 13, **13**
Telescopes 92, **92**
Test tubes 101, **101**
Theories 18
Thermometers 30, **31**, 86, **86**
Thorax 37, 125
Tigers **26-27**
Touch, sense of 13, **13**
Tree frogs 35, **45**
Tropical rain forests 62, **62**
Tundra 63, **63**
Turtles 46-47, **47**
Tyrannosaurs **76**

U
Uranus (planet) **95**

V
Vaccinations 30
Variables 16
Venus (planet) **94**
Vertebrates 37
Veterinarians 25, **25**
Vibrate 125
Viruses 31, 125
Vocal cords 107, 125
Volcanoes **20-21**, 78-79, **78-79**

W
Waves
   defined 125
   light 108-109, 125
   oceans 109, **109**
   sound 106-107, 109, 125
Weather **86-89**, 125
Western blood-red lady beetle **38-39**
Western tiger swallowtail butterfly **38-39**
Whales **29**, 74
Whale sharks 43, **43**
Wind 87
Wolves 55, **55**
Worms 59, **59**

X
X-ray machines 32-33, **33**

Y
Yeti crabs **85**

Z
Zoology see Animals

TO ALL THE CURIOUS YOUNG SCIENTISTS OUT THERE: KEEP ON EXPLORING! YOU ARE OUR HOPE. YOU ARE THE FUTURE. —KWZ

Published by Collins
An imprint of HarperCollins Publishers
1 Robroyston Gate,
Glasgow
G33 1JN
www.harpercollins.co.uk

HarperCollins Publishers
Macken House
39/40 Mayor Street Upper
Dublin 1
D01 C9W8
Ireland

© 2019 National Geographic Partners LLC. All rights reserved. NATIONAL GEOGRAPHIC KIDS and Yellow Border Design are trademarks of National Geographic Society, used under license.

First published 2019
This edition 2026

ISBN 9780008825164

10 9 8 7 6 5 4 3 2 1

All rights reserved. No part of this publication may be reproduced, stored in a retrieval system, or transmitted, in any form or by any means, electronic, mechanical, photocopying, recording or otherwise without the prior permission in writing of the publisher and copyright owners.

Without limiting the exclusive rights of any author, contributor or the publisher of this publication, any unauthorised use of this publication to train generative artificial intelligence (AI) technologies is expressly prohibited. HarperCollins also exercise their rights under Article 4(3) of the Digital Single Market Directive 2019/790 and expressly reserve this publication from the text and data mining exception.

The contents of this publication are believed correct at the time of printing. Nevertheless the publisher cannot accept responsibility for errors or omissions, changes in the detail given or for any expense or loss thereby caused.

HarperCollins does not warrant that any website mentioned in this title will be provided uninterrupted, that any website will be error free, that defects will be corrected, or that the website or the server that makes it available are free of viruses or bugs. For full terms and conditions please refer to the site terms provided on the website.

A catalogue record for this book is available from the British Library

Printed in India

If you would like to comment on any aspect of this book, please contact us at the above address or online.
natgeokidsbooks.co.uk
collins.reference@harpercollins.co.uk

Designed by Yay! Design

The publisher would like to acknowledge and thank early childhood learning specialists Barbara Bradley and Catherine D. Hughes for their expert insights and guidance. Many thanks also to project manager Grace Hill and researcher Michelle Harris for their invaluable help with this book.

Photo Credits

AL=Alamy Stock Photo; DT=Dreamstime; GI=Getty Images; IS=iStockphoto; MP=Minden Pictures; NGIC=National Geographic Image Collection; SS=Shutterstock

FRONT COVER: (UP LE), Tdway/SS; (UP CTR), Bogdan Ionescu/SS; (UP RT), James Laurie/SS; (CTR LE), Marques/SS; (CTR RT), Peter Kotoff/SS; (CTR RT inset), Heinrich Van Den Berg/DT; (LO LE), Andrey Armyagov/SS; (LO CTR), Fotos593/SS; (LO RT), Jgi/Daniel Grill/GI; **SPINE:** Sashkin/SS; **BACK COVER:** (UP RT), Brian J. Skerry/NGIC; **FRONT MATTER:** 1, Vchalup/DT; 2-3, Norbert Michalke/Imagebroker/Newscom; 4 (LO LE), Eric Isselee/SS; 4 (UP RT), The Image Bank/GI; 5 (UP RT), David Aguilar/NGIC; 5 (LO RT), Real444/GI; **CHAPTER 1:** 8-9, Peter Mason/GI; 10 (UP RT), Andrey Kuzmin/GI; 10 (LO), Stevecoleimages/GI; 11 (UP), First Class Photos Pty Ltd/SS; 11 (LO RT), R. Maximiliane/SS; 11 (LO LE), Sedmi/SS; 11 (LO RT), Andrew Rich/Richvintage/GI; 12 (UP), Sanchik/SS; 12 (LO), Patrick Foto/SS; 13 (UP), Wavebreakmedia/SS; 13 (CTR), Spfotocz/SS; 13 (LO), Rafal Olechowski/SS; 14 (LO LE), Photastic/SS; 14 (LO CTR), Windu/SS; 15 (UP), Eric Baccega/Nature Picture Library/MP; 15 (LO RT), Eric Isselee/SS; 16 (LO LE), Viktoria Gavrilina/SS; 16 (UP RT), Mark Thiessen/NGIC; 16 (UP RT), Mikephotos/DT; 16-17 (LO), Iurii Stepanov/SS; 17 (UP), Diana Taliun/SS; 17 (LO CTR), Summer Scrapbook/NGIC; 17 (LO RT), Fabika/SS; 17 (Polaroid), Nelson Marques/SS; 18 (LO CTR), Anna Kucherova/SS; 18-19 (CTR CTR), Ryan Smith/GI; 19 (UP), Kdow/IS/GI; 19 (CTR RT), Tracy Decoury/DT; 19 (LO), Hero Images/GI; 20 (LE), Erik Isakson/GI; 20 (RT), Jeremy Bishop/Science Photo Library/GI; 21 (UP), Katherine Feng/MP; 21 (CTR), Babak Tafreshi/NGIC; 21 (LO), Karim Agabi/Science Source; 22 (CTR), John Wollwerth/SS; 24, Mikephotos/DT; 25 (UP), Caiaimage/Paul Bradbury/GI; 25 (LO), Didesign021/SS; **CHAPTER 2:** 26-27, Nattanan726/SS; 28, Cathy Keifer/SS; 29 (UP RT), Yann-Hubert/GI; 29 (LO RT), Robert Christopher/GI; 29 (LO RT), Szasz-Fabian Jozsef/SS; 30, Ron Levine/GI; 31 (UP), Hero Images/GI; 31 (LO LE), Sirtravelalot/SS; 31 (LO CTR), Photodisc/NGIC; 32 (LE), Itsmejust/SS; 32 (RT), Gen Epic Solutions/SS; 35 (UP), Steve Gettle/MP; 35 (LO LE), Aleksey Stemmer/SS; 35 (LO RT), Eric Isselee/SS; 36, Rolf Nussbaumer/Nature Picture Library/MP; 37 (UP LE), Tsekhmister/SS; 37 (UP RT), Yusnizam Yusof/SS; 37 (LO RT), Daveallenphoto/DT; 38 (LE), Banditta Art/SS; 38-39, Artazum/SS; 38-39 (UP CTR), Don Farrall/GI; 38-39 (CTR CTR), Nnehring/IS/GI; 38-39 (CTR LE), Jennifer Bosvert/SS; 38-39 (UP LE), Karloss/SS; 38-39 (CTR RT), Tom Biegalski/SS; 38-39 (LO RT), Tea Maeklong/SS; 38-39 (CTR LE), Steve Bower/SS; 40, Glowimages/GI; 41 (UP LE), David Villegas Rios/SS; 41 (UP RT), Jiang Hongyan/SS; 41 (LO), Boris Pamikov/SS; 42-43, Tschuma417/GI; 43 (UP), Reinhard Dirscherl/FLPA/MP; 43 (CTR), Ken Kiefer 2/GI; 43 (LO), Ian Scott/SS; 44 (LO), David Roth/GI; 44 (UP), Martin Shields/GI; 45 (UP), Kathleen Finlay/Masterfile; 45 (LO), Kuttelvaserova Stuchelova/SS; 46 (UP), Lucas Bustamante/Nature Picture Library/MP; 46 (LO), Eric Isselee/SS; 47 (UP), Ch'ien Lee/MP; 47 (LO), Tim Zurowsk/GI; 48, William Leaman/AL; 49 (UP LE), Tim Laman/NGIC; 49 (CTR RT), Fieldwork/SS; 49 (LO RT), All_About_People/SS; 50 (CTR), Super Prin/SS; 50 (LO), Mark Miller Photos/GI; 51, Glass And Nature/SS; 52, Tono Balaguer/SS; 53 (UP LE), Jarrod Calati/SS; 53 (UP RT), D. Parer And E. Parer-Cook/MP; 53 (LO LE), Mitsuaki Iwago/MP; 53 (LO CTR), Mitsuaki Iwago/MP; 53 (LO RT), Tatyana Gladskikh/DT; 54 (UP), Johner Images/GI; 54 (LE), Christophe Courteau/Nature Picture Library; 55 (UP LE), Ajlber/IS/GI Plus; 55 (UP CTR), Anita Van Den Broek/SS; 55 (UP RT), Robert Mcgouey/GI; 55 (LO LE), Chris Fourie/IS/GI Plus; 55 (LO CTR), Lillian King/SS; 55 (LO RT), Lukas Blazek/DT; 56 (LO LE), Kidstock/GI; 56 (LO RT), Vavlt/IS/GI; 57 (UP LE), Rebecca Hale/NGIC; 57 (UP CTR LE), Rebecca Hale/NGIC; 57 (UP CTR RT), Rebecca Hale/NGIC; 57 (UP RT), Rebecca Hale/NGIC; 57 (LO), Laura Flugga/Huephotography/GI; 58 (LO LE), Alan Hopps/GI; 58 (RT), Asiseeit/GI; 59 (UP LE), Photographyfirm/SS; 59 (CTR RT), Smileus/SS; 59 (LO), Westend61 Gmbh/AL; 60-61, Image Source Salsa/AL; 61 (UP), Ignatius Tan/GI; 61 (CTR), Alex Mustard/Nature Picture Library; 61 (LO), Adriana Margarita Larios Arellano/SS; 62 (UP), Pete Oxford/MP; 62 (LO), Ben Sadd/FLPA/MP; 63 (UP), Krzysztof Dydynski/Lonely Planet Images/GI; 63 (LO), Jeff Schultz/Design Pics Inc/NGIC; 64, Jaguarblanco/IS/GI; 65 (UP), Luigi Masella/Eyeem/GI; 65 (LO), Rawpixel/SS; **CHAPTER 3:** 66-67, Marc Ward/Stocktrek Images/GI; 68, Johnson Space Center/NASA; 69, Juergen Faelchle/SS; 70 (LE), Sumit Buranarothtrakul/SS; 70-71 (CTR), Gary Schultz/Design Pics/GI; 71 (LO CTR RT), Michal812/SS; 71 (LO CTR RT), Jxfzsy/IS/GI; 71 (LO), Oleg63sam/DT; 72 (CTR LE), Anetapics/SS; 72 (LO LE), Tatiana Popova/SS; 72 (UP RT), Ingvald Kaldhussater/DT; 72 (CTR RT), Niglaynik/SS; 72 (LO RT), Breakermaximus/SS; 72-73 (UP CTR LE), Foottoo/SS; 73 (UP RT), Chris Hepburn/GI; 72 (CTR LE), Andrey Armyagov/SS; 73 (CTR CTR), Debr22pics/SS; 73 (LO LE), Diyana Dimitrova/SS; 73 (LO CTR), Studiovin/SS; 73 (LO RT), Leonard Zhukovsky/SS; 74, Richard Barnes/NGIC; 75 (UP), Millard H. Sharp/Science Source; 75 (LO), Science Stock Photography/Science Source; 76-77, Patrick Aventurier/Gamma-Rapho/GI; 76 (inset), Sabena Jane Blackbird/AL; 78, Ammit Jack/SS; 79 (UP), Peter Carsten/NGIC; 79 (CTR), Andrea Danti/SS; 79 (LO), Ralf Lehmann/SS; 80-81, Imagine China/Newscom; 81, Pacific Press/AL; 82, Arnulf Husmo/GI; 83 (UP LE), Dudarev Mikhail/SS; 83 (RT), Frantisekhojdysz/SS; 84, Jeff Rotman/GI; 85 (UP), Science Source/GI; 85 (LO LE), David Shale/Nature Picture Library/MP; 85 (LO RT), Norbert Wu/MP; 86-87, Suwin/SS; 86 (LO), Digital Light Source/Uig Via GI; 87 (LO), Martina I. Meyer/SS; 88, Jim Reed/Corbis/GI; 88 (UP RT), Jean-Paul Nacivet/GI; 90-91, Ethan Welty/GI; 91 (inset), Eric Kruszewski/NGIC; 92, Lester Lefkowitz/GI; 92-93, Valentin Armianu/DT; 94-95, Bsip/Uig Via GI; 94 (LO), Johnson Space Center/Nasa; 95 (LO RT), Jet Propulsion Laboratory/NASA; **CHAPTER 4:** 96-97, Michael Carver/GI; 98, Blend Images - John Lund/Drew Kelly/GI; 99 (UP), Romrodphoto/SS; 99 (LO), Heinzteh/SS; 100, Wavebreakmedia/SS; 101 (UP), NGIC; 101 (LO), Jgi/Jamie Grill/GI; 102, Jgi/GI; 103 (UP), Henn Photography/GI; 103 (LO), B.A.E. Inc./AL; 104, David Malan/GI; 105, Bartosz Hadyniak/GI; 106 (UP), Nicolasmccomber/GI; 106 (LO), Davydenko Yuliia/SS; 106-107 (CTR), Elizabethsalleebauer/GI; 107 (RT), Anton Havelaar/SS; 108, Teresa Short/GI; 109 (UP), David Parker/Science Photo Library/GI; 109 (CTR), Paul Topp/DT; 109 (LO), Adam Gault/GI; 110, Andria Patino/GI; 111 (UP), Oorka/IS/GI; 111 (LO), Yuganov Konstantin/SS; 112 (UP LE), Hurst Photo/SS; 112 (UP CTR), Kubrak78/IS/GI; 112 (UP RT), Nanta Samran/SS; 112 (CTR LE), Denis Kovin/SS; 112 (CTR CTR), Elnur/SS; 112 (LO LE), Ukki Studio/SS; 112 (LO CTR), Picsfive/SS; 112 (LO RT), Christian Delbert/SS; 113 (UP LE), NGIC; 113 (UP CTR), Nadiia Korol/SS; 113 (UP RT), Krolya25/SS; 113 (CTR LE), Jannoon028/SS; 113 (CTR CTR), Gmstockstudio/SS; 113 (LO LE), Dmitry Vinogradov/SS; 113 (LO CTR), Mikhail Rulkov/SS; 113 (LO RT), 3dmi/SS; **CHAPTER 5:** 114-115, Muratart/SS; 116 (LE), Interfoto/AL; 116-117 (CTR), Mircea Costina/SS; 117 (UP), Diane Miller/GI; 117 (LO), Zeynep Demir/SS; 118 (UP LE), Saginbay/SS; 118 (LO LE), Chesky/SS; 118 (LO RT), Tony Gray/Kennedy Space Center/NASA; 119 (UP), Jason Patrick Ross/SS; 119 (LO), Sofiaworld/SS; 120 (UP), Massawfoto/SS; 120-121 (UP), Prokrida/SS; 120-121 (CTR), NGIC; 120 (inset), Donsmith/AL; 120 (LO), Urfin/SS; 121 (CTR RT), Goir/SS; 121 (LO), NGIC; **BACK MATTER:** 122, Tory Zimmerman/Toronto Star Via GI; 123 (UP), Karidesign/SS; 123 (LO), Monkey Business Images Ltd/DT; 125, SliNGShot/Corbis/GI